CW00747089

The Third Space

Using Life's Little Transitions to Find Balance and Happiness

Dr Adam Fraser
Foreword by Stephen Lundin, author of Fish!

16

EasyRead Large

Copyright Page from the Original Book

A William Heinemann book
Published by Random House Australia Pty Ltd
Level 3, 100 Pacific Highway, North Sydney NSW 2060
www.randomhouse.com.au

First published by William Heinemann in 2012

Copyright © Adam Fraser 2012

The moral right of the author has been asserted.

All rights reserved. No part of this book may be reproduced or transmitted by any person or entity, including internet search engines or retailers, in any form or by any means, electronic or mechanical, including photocopying (except under the statutory exceptions provisions of the Australian *Copyright Act 1968*), recording, scanning or by any information storage and retrieval system without the prior written permission of Random House Australia.

Addresses for companies within the Random House Group can be found at www.randomhouse.com.au/offices.

National Library of Australia
Cataloguing-in-Publication Entry

Fraser, Adam.
The third space / Adam Fraser.

ISBN 978 1 74275 386 7 (pbk.)

Self-actualization (Psychology)
Achievement motivation.
Work-life balance.
Behavior modification.
Self-help techniques.

158.1

Cover design and internal diagrams by Jennifer Sheahan
Internal design and typesetting by Midland Typesetters, Australia
Printed in Australia by Griffin Press, an accredited ISO AS/NZS 14001:2004 Environmental Management System printer

Random House Australia uses papers that are natural, renewable and recyclable products and made from wood grown in sustainable forests. The logging and manufacturing processes are expected to conform to the environmental regulations of the country of origin.

This optimized ReadHowYouWant edition contains the complete, unabridged text of the original publisher's edition. Other aspects of the book may vary from the original edition.

Copyright © 2010 Accessible Publishing Systems PTY, Ltd. ACN 085 119 953

The text in this edition has been formatted and typeset to make reading easier and more enjoyable for ALL kinds of readers. In addition the text has been formatted to the specifications indicated on the title page. The formatting of this edition is the copyright of Accessible Publishing Systems Pty Ltd.

Set in 16 pt. Verdana

ReadHowYouWant partners with publishers to provide books for ALL Kinds of Readers. For more information about Becoming A (RHYW) Registered Reader and to find more titles in your preferred format, visit:
<u>www.readhowyouwant.com</u>

TABLE OF CONTENTS

Dr Adam Fraser was a scientist in a previous life, studying psychology and physiology. After growing tired of academica he stepped into the world of business and became one of Australia's most sought-after keynote speakers and consultants, all the time staying at the cutting edge by continuing his research. During his career he has worked with a huge range of people, including elite-level athletes, Special Forces soldiers and CEOs of billion-dollar companies. In the last five years he has delivered more than 600 presentations to over 50,000 people. In addition, Dr Adam is CEO of The Glucose Club, a company that guides and supports individuals into a lifestyle to prevent or improve existing diabetes. He is the author of the bestseller *Sugar Daddy.*

'In a clearly written treatise with insightful anecdotes and personal stories, Dr Adam Fraser has successfully created a manual for managing the "in-between" moments that can throw many of us off balance. By taking a novel approach to handling the often-ignored "Third Space", the author gives us the tools to survive in an increasingly stress-filled world of competing responsibilities.'

–Marshall Goldsmith, million-selling author of the *New York Times* bestsellers *MOJO* and *What Got You Here Won't Get You There*

'This certainly isn't yet another self-help book. Adam is inspirationally on the ball: managing the Third Space equals happiness and fulfilment. This book is universal in its application, whoever we are and whatever we do.'

–Robert Marriott, Head of Human Resources, Bank of Tokyo-Mitsubishi UFJ

'*The Third Space* is not your everyday self-help book. Reading it helped me improve my relationship with my teenage daughter, become a better role model for her and make my evenings at home a more pleasant experience for the whole family, including me!'

–Nieves Murray, Chief Executive, IRT

'What it takes to survive and thrive in the 21st century requires more than a positive outlook or personal discipline – tomorrow's executives need to reprogram their mindset to be able to constantly shift between roles and situations. *The Third Space* is your guidebook to the mental agility essential to being a successful leader, and more importantly, a successful human being!'

–Mike Walsh, globally renowned futurist, CEO of the innovation research lab, Tomorrow, and best-selling author of *Futuretainment*

'In a world where the standard response to "how are you?" is "busy", Dr Adam Fraser's *The Third Space* has universal appeal, giving clear and practical suggestions for how to get the most out of life's experiences.'

–Angela Tsoukatos, General Manager of Customer Services, Sydney Water

'Happiness is elusive. It's something we dream of achieving one day – when life slows down and we're more in control. But *The Third Space* shows us that true happiness, fulfilment and balance are achievable through mindfully stepping into the Third Space and taking control of every aspect of our lives.'

–Sue Hollis, CEO, Traveledge

'Adopting the principles and practices of the Third Space will change your life! A brilliant "must read" for every busy person.'

–Avril Henry, Managing Director, Avril Henry Pty Ltd

'*The Third Space* is a book that tackles one of the biggest problems facing all professionals. This problem costs not only time and money, but more importantly it affects our loved ones and our personal happiness. Thanks, Dr Fraser for having the foresight and research to write such marvellous book.'

–Dale Beaumont, author of 16 bestselling books and founder of Business Blueprint

For my wonderful wife, Christine, who makes each day worth showing up for.

Foreword

BY STEPHEN LUNDIN

Professor of Business, Griffith University

The fishmongers at the world-famous Pike Place Fish Market in Seattle frequently refer to the 'spaces' they occupy and the role this has played in their success, so I am familiar with the concept of 'space'. I still found *The Third Space* provocative. Adam Fraser uses spaces to refer to the transition between life's episodes. These transitions can be measured in seconds or hours, but they are all important to a happy life. In this book, Adam has made a clear and compelling case for the importance of actively managing life's transitions by choosing your mindset, emotions and behaviour as you show up in the next episode. The material here is important, the stories helpful to understanding it. I referred to this book as provocative. Let me explain.

I read about the importance of the Third Space to personal well-being, a wonderful gift that Adam gives you, and found myself thinking about the Third Space in customer service and in leadership. Actually, there were a lot more, but these two were the most interesting.

Carr Hagerman, my friend, colleague and co-author of the book *Top Performer*[1], spent much of his life as a costume street performer. We met when Carr expressed an interest in conducting some of the FISH! Camps we held in the early days of the FISH! Phenomenon. I learned a great deal from Carr over the years, especially about how to show up in the space you share with a customer. We were at the headquarters of a major retail firm that had experienced falling customer service scores. After meeting with them, it was easy to see why many other firms benchmarked against this company. They had one of the most sophisticated approaches to customer service we had ever seen. Carr started questioning them about the transition between the morning meeting – a time spent reviewing various customer service protocols – and entering the store. After listening politely to the polished professional presentation, he made a simple but profound suggestion. He said, 'When the agents go out on the floor to work with customers, tell them to forget all the rules and protocols of customer service and just show up as an authentic human being.' Things improved dramatically. The customer service mindset was interfering with the most important element in the equation, the human being.

Leadership is about the moments. The ingredients of leadership are qualities like honesty, empathy, courage, compassion, caring, and candour. Adam talks about the transitions between work spaces as the manager moves from one setting to another: meeting is followed by individual contact which is followed by quick chat with the boss, and so it goes. I believe

Henry Mintzberg was the first to talk about management as a series of short bursts. It seems to me that the transitions are critical to leadership. The biggest part of leadership is simply showing up as a leader. To do this means managing the transitions, and managing the Third Space.

Stephen Lundin, author of *FISH! A Remarkable Way to Boost Morale and Improve Results.*[2]

Chapter 1

Introduction: mind the gap

For decades we have been talking about, researching and striving for stress management and work-life balance. All the while our stress levels are skyrocketing and balance is being ripped out from under us. The minutes in our day are so jam-packed, a cancelled meeting is greeted with the grateful relief our parents' generation used to feel about a two-week holiday. The techniques we embraced have failed us. It's time we woke up and adopted a new approach. This book is that new approach. An approach that moulds and fuses with your busy lifestyle rather than trying to battle it, tie it up and constrain it.

Why do we need it? Well, it's not a pretty picture. Eighty-two per cent of Australians hate or do not like their job.[1] Globally, this number is 81 per cent (another area in which Australia is leading the world). Only seven per cent of the population feel that they are thriving in the areas of their lives such as health, social life, career, finance and community.[2] Depression rates have risen by a factor of ten in the last 50 years.[3]

One of the reasons for this bad news is that many people feel like their life is out of control, as though they are handcuffed to a roller-coaster stuck on repeat. Let me give you an example.

EXECUTIVE, PARTNER AND MOTHER OUT OF CONTROL

Karen burst into the room, swinging the door open so hard it smashed into the wall behind and shook the room. She was moving fast and talking even faster and hit me with a wave of energy. Instantly I knew this was going to be no ordinary coaching session. This 40-something, slim, athletic woman was an immaculately dressed, miniature hurricane.

While she exuded energy, it was not focused: it seemed to spray around the room like a hose turned on and let go. I asked her to have a seat. Her backside barely touched the chair before she jumped back up again, diving headfirst into her bag. She rattled off a muffled apology: 'Sorry, sorry, I have to send this email,' as her arms gesticulated wildly.

If you hooked this woman up to a generator, she could power a small nation in Eastern Europe.

I asked how I could help her. She looked up from the BlackBerry that she was pounding away on and, while frantically chewing on a pen, said, 'I need you to stop me from having a complete mental breakdown.'

Wow, don't hold back, lady.

'I'm serious. I have been the CEO of this company for one year and it's killing me. My family hates me. I'm failing at being a mother. The board says I'm not performing to my potential. At this rate, in another year I will be dead or in an asylum.'

Trying to recover from the barrage, I asked, 'How would you describe your life?'

She replied, 'I feel like the hamster's dead but the wheel's still spinning.'

Before the meeting, I had found out that Karen was brilliant, with an amazing business mind. Her staff would lie down in traffic for her: they loved her and would follow her anywhere. Yet she was falling apart. For the next 50 minutes she told me everything that was wrong with her life, whipping herself into an increasing frenzy. Towards the end of the hour, I said, 'What I want you to do for the next week is to observe how you "show up" for each part of your life – each task, role and environment. How do you "show up" for work, how do you show up for home, how do you show up for a leadership meeting? Every time you transition into a new task, environment or role – friend, leader, partner, parent – ask yourself, 'How am I "showing up"?'

'What do you mean "show up"?' was her aggressive reply.

'What I mean is, what thoughts, emotions and behaviour do you bring to every new role, task or environment in your life?'

She seemed dissatisfied with my request and was not trying hard to conceal it.

My reply was stern: 'This is not some fluffy exercise. I need you to do it and I need you to do it well.'

One week later I turned up for our next meeting, curious about what kind of homework Karen would turn in. I barely had time to sit down before Karen exploded into the room.

'I did your little exercise! Do you know what I realised? When I walk into work in the morning, do you know what I say to myself? "You're a bad mother because you're not at home with your kids. You are outsourcing raising your kids to strangers, and it will come back to bite you in a couple of years." Do you know how that makes me feel? GUILTY! Because of this, I can't focus and I'm stressed out. But then I go home and do you know what I say to myself when I walk in the door? "You're a bad CEO because you are not at work. All the other CEOs are still at work. How do you expect to compete with them when you're at home mucking around with the family?" Do you know how that makes me feel? I will tell you: GUILTY! Because of that, I can't focus on my family and all I can think about is work. I keep checking my BlackBerry, I am not present and my family knows it. Do you know what I got from your little exercise? It made me realise that I am freakin' miserable in every area of my life.'

Have you ever felt the same?

Do you feel that you simply react to each part of your life rather than have control over it? Do you feel as though you have all these different roles but you keep no one in any of them happy?

If you answered 'yes' to these questions, this book is for you.

This book is all about how we transition between the different areas of our life and how we can use these transitions to find happiness and balance.

LIFE IS A SERIES OF DIFFERENT ROLES

Does this sound familiar?

You're a senior manager sitting at your desk, designing the PowerPoint slides for your presentation to the board, when the phone rings. It's Human Resources. They want to meet with you due to a complaint of bullying against one of your direct reports. As you head out of the room you think about how you knew he was a bloody lawsuit waiting to happen.

You try, without success, to put out the fire at the meeting. In fact you only manage to add fuel to the inferno-in-waiting.

As you leave HR you realise you're ten minutes late for a brainstorming session with operations about optimising the company's supply chain. You contribute nothing as your thoughts are consumed with rehearsing the script you'll have to deliver to the CEO when you tell her that your number one sales manager has been accused of bullying.

Your PA enters the room with a note for you, in-terrupting your mental holiday. It says that one of your high-volume customers is furious about the delivery of a faulty product. You race out of the room and try to talk them out of jumping ship to your competition.

In what seems like the blink of an eye but is actually an hour later, you're behind the wheel. It's your one day in the week to pick up the kids and chauffeur them to their extra-curricular activities. You pick one up from school and one from day care and listen to one of them complain that Willow doesn't want to be his friend anymore while the other moans about her homework.

You get home and are greeted by a messy house and a partner who has had a 'crap' day and expects you to make it better. You listen to them for an hour while they tell you about how much of a jerk their manager is and how they don't get enough recognition for their hard work.

While your partner makes dinner, you turn schoolteacher and help the kids with their homework, all the while trying to access the part of your brain that paid attention in long division.

You clean up dinner and prepare for the next day by opening the diary on your computer. An email pops up from your manager that says he doesn't think you are being the inspiring leader you need to be. Thanks for that! After mentally fashioning a voodoo doll of him and sticking it full of pins, you open up the third module of your MBA course, the one that you enrolled in because you were lacking a challenge in life. You spend 15 minutes re-reading the same paragraph because your numbed brain is demanding time off and then opt for a glass of red and a brainless TV show.

Finally, you pour yourself into bed. You roll over in a near-vegetative state to face your partner, who gives you the look that says 'tonight is the night'. After you regretfully decline, they launch into a 45-minute keynote on the fact that they have needs and you aren't meeting them, that relationships are about give and take, intimacy is important and you need to put in more effort. After fighting the urge to suffocate them with your pillow, you fall into a blissful coma. You emerge drooling from unconsciousness an hour later: a small child is standing next to you, saying, 'I had a nightmare. I think there's a monster in my room.'

You take him by the hand and walk him back to bed while exploring your memories, trying to work out what idiot told you children are the best thing that could ever happen to you. As you tuck him in, you are hoping a huge monster jumps out of the cupboard and decapitates you. Back in your own bed, the alarm clock flashes 4.30am. Great. Only one hour and 30 minutes till it all starts again.

After reading this you may feel like a good lie-down to recover. The reality is that this is the life of many people today. Whether or not your activities are identical to those mentioned, they are likely to be just as diverse, constant and challenging.

Did anything exceptional or life-changing happen on this day? Did our senior manager move house? Did they change jobs? Did they start a new relationship?

No.

Their day was a series of micro-transitions as they moved among the different roles, tasks and environments of their life.

IMPORTANCE OF MICRO-TRANSITIONS

Micro-transitions are, in fact, what life is all about. However, we make the mistake of focusing too much on the major transitions in life: moving in with your partner; handling the new restructure at work after a major round of redundancies; or adjusting to life with a new baby in the house. Major transitions are very real but relatively infrequent. In fact, most of everyday life consists of micro-transitions. It's the effectiveness of *these* transitions, not the major ones, that actually determines how happy we are. Whether we will end up needing a new house, job or relationship, and how we will embrace or otherwise handle those large transitions, is very much determined by how we handle the many and varied micro-transitions of our lives.

How are you currently handling your micro-transitions? Are you effectively transitioning between each role you fulfil? I can guarantee that if you improve the quality of your micro-transitions, you are going to be less stressed, have more balance and be happier in your life.

Our greatest challenge in life today and within the next decade will not be the amount of work we have to do, as it has peaked and shows no sign of declining. Instead, the challenge is the way we transition between different tasks, roles and environments for maximised performance. Our world is more out of control than ever before, with us transitioning faster than at any other time in history. In this turbo-charged world the secret to finding balance, peace and happiness exists in these transitional gaps. In other words we have to start minding the gap.

WE MOVE BETWEEN SPACES

I refer to these roles, environments and different tasks as 'Spaces'. We spend our day transitioning between different Spaces. The First Space is the role/environment/task you are in right now: namely reading this book. The Second Space is the role/environment/task you are transitioning into. For example, you might be about to go into a sales conference or have your annual performance review or take part in a parent-teacher conference. The Third Space is the transitional gap in between the First and

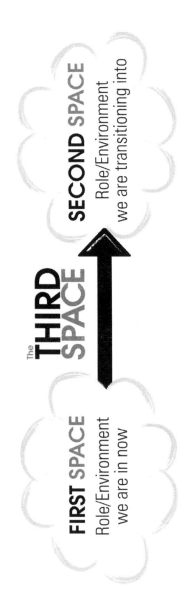

Second. What we do in this transitional space will determine our level of success in the Second space. It is the gap where we learn from and recover from the First Space while preparing for optimal performance in the Second Space.

When I worked with athletes we called this transitional gap 'mental rehearsal'. As they moved through the Third Space, transitioning into training or competition, they would think about how they wanted to feel, how they wanted to perform, and what they wanted to focus on, when they entered the Second Space. This was a very effective technique because it helped them assume the right mindset for the best chance of success in that next space.

However, when I started working with non-athletes, I discovered that they did not take advantage of this gap. Instead they would rush through, ignoring the Third Space and assuming a mindset that was not conducive to the Second Space they were moving into.

In my work as a researcher, consultant and coach I have seen firsthand how devastating it can be to people's lives when they don't get the Third Space right. I see salespeople get rejected and carry that rejection into the next sales situation. I see people have a bad day at work and take it out on their family. I've seen people turn up to a presentation and do a terrible job because they carried in with them a fearful and distracted mindset.

In this book, I will show how you can use the Third Space to allow you to 'show up' with the right mindset to make that next interaction a success. The ability to transition rapidly – to inhabit the Third Space fully and effectively and to step up and handle the next space – is one of the most important skills you need to survive and thrive in both your work and personal lives.

Based on my research and my experience presenting this concept to business audiences, *The Third Space* is the first book to explore the concept of micro-transitions. Many books have looked at how we handle large transitions such as a new leadership role or career path, or how to handle being retrenched. However, none of these looks at how we cope with the ongoing demands of diverse roles and an urgent world that expects instant responses.

This book will help you 'mind the gap'.

SUMMARY

- Stress and depression levels are rising. People feel their lives are out of control.
- A new approach to stress management and work-life balance is to no longer focus on trying to reduce the volume of work but rather look at how we transition between the different tasks, environments and roles we fulfil.
- These tasks, environments and roles are referred to as Spaces. The First Space is the role/environment/task we are in right now. The Second Space is the role/environment/task we are about to move into.
- The Third Space is the transitional gap in between the First and Second spaces. The focus of this book is how we can use the Third Space to gain more balance and happiness. The way we do this is to use this gap to learn from the First Space and to

adopt a mindset that gets us the best possible outcome in the Second Space.

Chapter 2

Give me some space

We often hear that people make their minds up about others in the first 30 seconds of meeting. However, this may be a gross overestimate. In his book *Blink,* Malcolm Gladwell suggests that we make decisions about people and situations almost instantaneously and then spend the rest of the time justifying that assumption.[1] He talks about a concept called 'thin-slicing', which is a snap judgement based on a thin slice of information/experience. With the increase in working hours, workload and roles we fulfil, 'thin-slicing' is more important than it has ever been. What this means for us is that when we transition, we have to be on the ball because it's *game on!* Imagine if Karen entered an important sales meeting the way she came to see me. Would her client have considered her competent, trustworthy – even sane?

Our world has accelerated so much that the time we get in each space has become compressed. What you do with these small spaces determines the quality of your life. If you don't make the most of each space you are missing out on your life.

RELATIONSHIPS

The average Australian knowledge worker is 3.6 times more likely to give priority to their work role than their family role.[2] An insurance company called Ensure commissioned Fly Research to survey 1000 people over the age of 18 in the UK. The results showed that 20 per cent of couples only spoke for 15 minutes each day, with 27 per cent noting that they only have a proper conversation with their partner on the weekend. Forty-one per cent admitted to using text messaging, email or social media to communicate rather than talking. What would grow a relationship more – 40 minutes of cuddling on the couch, connecting with each other's day, or receiving a text message saying 'I♥u'? The average American only spends 40 minutes socialising with friends each day,[3] yet they spend close to three hours each day watching TV. In fact only 38 per cent of Americans invite their friends over for dinner once or more each year.[4] Even our relationships are reduced to these small spaces of interactions.

A great parent is one who grasps onto each space with both hands and interacts with their child with love, compassion and joy. Spaces can be wasted when we see our children as a source of frustration, something that simply gets in the way of our lives. The result is an interaction ruled by contempt and aggression. A great partner is one who spends each space with optimism, empathy and respect. We waste those spaces when we criticise our partners or treat them as emotional punching bags to relieve our frustration and personal shortcomings. A great friend is one who spends those spaces being supportive, fun and inspiring. We waste each space when we are petty and judgemental.

If you manage people at work, how much time do you get to spend with your team? The answer is probably very little. What are you doing with each space you have with your team? A great leader in an organisation is one who manages and leads in each space. They seek to understand and inspire, they have empathy and they put their team into a state of calm focus. Poor leaders are frustrated with their team in each space. They tend to use anger, they are judgemental and they may try to make up for it by taking the team out at the end of the year for a boozy lunch. Poor leaders waste each precious space.

SMALL SPACES CAN MAKE YOU A CHAMPION

Managing each space well not only improves your interactions: the technique can also improve your performance.

Following their arrival home from the Beijing Olympics, I had the pleasure of facilitating a session with some of the Australian Olympic team. My role was to draw out information from the team and manage questions from the audience.

One of the participants was Steve Hooker, who won the gold medal in the pole vault. My question to him was this: 'Steve, in Athens (2004) you came 28th in the world. Four years later you won the gold. What did you do in those four years to get that quantum leap in performance?' His response was profound. Steve said that he had always done the big things right: trained hard, ate well and worked on his technique. However, he realised that he didn't do the small things right, such as taking time out each day to relax, working on his mental focus, meditating, monitoring his self-talk and improving his emotional control. Steve began to dedicate some space each day to the seemingly small things. He kept this up every day for four years. Steve said that to move from 'really good' to 'exceptional', you need to consistently do the small things day in and day out. In other words, you need to take advantage of each space.

In his book *The Power of Full Engagement,* Jim Loehr[5] studied top tennis players. Interestingly, he discovered that what separated the elite players from the great players was what they did in between the points rather than during the point itself. He found that the best players had very specific routines be-tween points, while lower-ranked players had no such routine. The best players used the gap between points to recover more effectively from the previous point and to better prepare themselves for the upcoming point. Specifically, they cleared their brain of the thoughts and judgements around the previous point, and then shifted into relaxation by slowing down their breathing. This in turn calmed their emotions and reduced the chance of them feeling anger and frustration. Finally, they would focus on the next point and prepare for it optimistically. While it doesn't sound like much and it may only last for 16 seconds, doing it hundreds of times in a match had a huge accumulative effect. In other words, it was how the player used the Third Space between points that determined his or her success.

THE ORIGIN OF THE THIRD SPACE

One afternoon in 2008, my mobile phone rang in the foyer of the Vibe Hotel in North Sydney. The voice on the other end of the line was very familiar. It was the voice of a Special Forces soldier I knew very well called Mike.

Mike is over 180 centimetres tall, 90 kilograms and as fit as a human being can get. He has been all over the world, has been under live enemy fire countless times, and has acted as personal bodyguard to prime ministers. He has seen and done things that you and I can barely comprehend.

While his voice was familiar on this day, what was unfamiliar was his tone of voice. It was one of fear, panic and helplessness. I said, 'Mike, you sound terrible. Where are you?'

He replied, 'I'm at home.'

'Home? What are you doing at home? I thought you were in the Middle East.'

'I've left the army.'

Hesitantly, I asked, '...Do THEY know you've left the army?'

'Yeah, it's fine. I left a couple of months ago.'

'Well are you okay? You just sound terrible.'

'No Ads, I am not okay. I'm freaking out. I have a situation that is out of control. I don't know what to do and I seriously think I'm having a nervous breakdown.'

Upon hearing this I started to freak out, thinking he might have Post Traumatic Stress Disorder.

I said, 'Look, mate. Just tell me what's going on.'

He took a deep breath and said, 'The problem is that Raquel has gone back to work and I am looking after the three kids ... It is the toughest thing I've ever done. It makes running ops in the Middle East feel like a walk in the park.'

I immediately burst out laughing.

'No, you don't understand,' he said. 'It's relentless. It doesn't stop. There's no time out, no down time, no rest. It just never ends. I joined a mothers' group for support, but they picked on me so much I had to leave. Women can be so cruel.'

At this point I heard a baby cry in the background.

He said in a hushed tone, 'Do you hear that noise? It never stops. I swear I can hear them in my sleep. If they're not hitting each other they are destroying something. I just change nappies all day. I see what I feed them. More comes out than goes in. I mean, the physics of that doesn't even add up.'

Then, the most unbelievable line. 'Look, I've been calling around a couple of private security companies to see if I could go back to Baghdad for a bit of time out.'

I was floored. Time out in Baghdad! You know you have stress in your life when you have to go to a war-torn country to relax.

How could someone so strong, so mentally tough, who has been pushed to the brink of what a human being can stand, come home to his family to be surrounded by loved ones and have a complete meltdown?

I began my search for the answer. First of all I looked deeper into Mike's situation. Why was he struggling so much? In simple terms, the transition was far too abrupt and severe. Only weeks earlier, he was rappelling down the side of a building or designing an operation to protect a group of engineers from a possible terrorist attack. In the blink of an eye he found himself sipping lattes with a group of mothers and talking about Tom Cruise and Katie Holmes. The result was that his mindset didn't match the space he was in. It wasn't that he was incapable of being a great father; rather, he had not transitioned into it correctly.

Over the coming months Mike started to turn it around. He learned how to 'show up' to suit his environment. How did he do this? The first step was to realise that there was a loss, that he would miss the adrenaline and, most importantly, his fellow soldiers. He had to acknowledge that fact and talk to people about what he was going through. The second step was to acknowledge that he had no direction. He simply did not know what type of father he wanted to be or what sort of life he wanted to lead. Being a high-performance person, he needed clear goals and something to work towards. In response, he enrolled at university to pursue a new career. He read books on being a better father and implemented the suggested techniques. He threw himself into exercise and took up the sports that his kids were playing so he could train with them. He had a clear intention about what sort of life he wanted to lead and how he wanted to act.

The change in him was immense; today he is an outstanding father and husband. What's the difference? He took steps to close down the First Space – being a Special Forces soldier (later in the book I refer to this as Reflect), and he had a clear intention and goal for the Second Space – being a stay-at-home dad (later in the book I refer to this as Reset). He aligned his mindset to the Second Space. In effect, he used the Third Space to 'show up' right.

A SOLDIER'S GREATEST CHALLENGE

Following this interaction, I started talking to a number of people in the armed forces. I asked them what their biggest challenge as a soldier was. Unsurprisingly, one of their biggest challenges was returning home after being away. Just like Mike, the reason was that their day job and their home life were incredibly different. Soldiers struggled to transition from one environment to the next.

Why? Think about it: the mindset they need as a soldier is completely different from the mindset they need as a partner, parent or civilian. Due to the huge gulf between these worlds, they struggle to move between them. Many of them told me, 'I don't find it hard to be away from home doing the job. The hard part is when I come home. For the first couple of weeks I really struggle reconnecting with the family because I have to think, feel and act very differently to when I'm away being a soldier. In fact, for a couple of weeks I feel like a stranger in my own home.' Others said: 'We go off and do things you can't even imagine, then they drop us home and we're supposed to cuddle our kids and take out the garbage. It's so hard to move between those worlds.' Family members, too, commented on the difficulty of having their loved ones return. The family gets used to their absence and when they come home they upset the routine.

With Mike, it wasn't that he lacked the ability to be a stay-at-home dad. It was simply that this transition was so great. The two spaces required him to think, feel and act very differently. Initially, Mike did not tap into the Third Space. He didn't effectively use the gap to prepare himself for the transition into his home environment.

During my research I received the following letter from another former soldier, John Ronan.

I was deployed on 'Op Belisi' in Bougainville for almost six months as part of the peace monitoring process.

During that time, the Australian Army Psychology Corps provided the troops with a booklet which provided tips on how to relate and stay in contact with your family while you are away. This booklet also gave you tips on how to transition back to home life upon your return. One tip was to write letters home to your children, as this was something special for them and they would still feel part of a family. But the best tip is to realise, when you return home, that your wife has been running the household as an individual and you should feel your way back into the family structure rather than come home trying to run the show. When I came home, I stood back and asked my wife what I needed to do for her. I really acted as a visitor in my own home rather than being the boss. I took time to observe the new routines and rituals in the house and endeavoured to blend in with them rather than try to change them. It worked a treat!

In all my 21 years in the army, this would have to be by far the best bit of advice I've ever received.

John used the Third Space masterfully to transition effectively into the Second Space.

Coming home from the army is clearly a major transition. However, this experience led me to realise that we make hundreds of micro-transitions in our day-to-day life. The micro-transitions occur when we move between different roles, tasks and environments, whose uniqueness requires us to think, feel and act differently.

I spoke to a policeman about micro-transitions. He told me a heartbreaking story: when he was a young and relatively new officer, this policeman had to tell a middle-aged couple that their three children had been killed in a car accident. 'I was 21, for heaven's sake. How the hell was I supposed to go home and live my life after that? Nothing in my police training prepared me to transition home after that.'

I asked how he had coped. His reply: 'Simple. I just went and drank until I stopped thinking about it.'

I worked with some miners whose jobs were fly-in fly-out. They worked for two weeks at the mines and then came home for two weeks. They said the hardest part of the job was transitioning home.

'I'm away for two weeks where I share a room with three stinky, sweaty men. When I get home it takes me four days to get civilised. I have a few good days, then I spend the rest of the time stressing about having to go back to work. I just really struggle transitioning between these two environments because they are so incredibly different.'

What do these examples have in common? People's quality of life suffered because of their inability to effectively manage micro-transitions in their life.

Clearly, micro-transitions are important. Transitioning poorly can have a devastating impact on our quality of life. If we transition effectively between every new role, task and environment, we feel more in control, have better relationships and greater happiness. Great leaders have the ability to transition from a situation that is personally demoralising for them to a meeting with their team members, without taking it out on them. Great salespeople have the ability to transition from a sales meeting in which the client tells them their product is terrible, to the next sales meeting without carrying that negative baggage with them. A great parent has the ability to have a frustrating day full of disappointment and setbacks and to then go home and not take the day out on their family.

In a way, you could say that transitions are like checking in your luggage at the airport. When you transition you need to leave your baggage in another place. However, that's only half of the picture. The Third Space is also about showing up with the right mindset to suit the role, task or environment that you are moving into.

CHILDREN NEED MICRO-TRANSITIONS

I recently discovered that managing micro-transitions is not only important for adults but also for children. My daughter Isabella has always had a strong personality and is very wilful (she inherited this from her mother). We'd always struggled moving her from one task or environment to another. Trying to get her off the swings at the park and into the pram was often like trying to wrestle a bear. She would protest and refuse to move. One day, I thought I'd see if the Third Space could work for her. So what we started to do was talk about the transition that was coming next. 'Bella, we're about to go home for dinner. In a couple of minutes we have to get off the swing and get in the pram so we can go home for dinner. Mmm ... yummy dinner.' We would literally count it down. 'Ten more swings to go, then we have to get off and into the pram.' It worked a treat. We did it with every micro-transition she made. 'After you eat that we are going to have a bath. Yay bath time! You love the bath, don't you? We can play with all your toys and splash around.' Her behaviour and capacity to handle transitions improved out of sight because we gave her time to process and adjust to the next activity coming her way. Previously we would say, 'Okay, Bella, time to go home,' and quickly move her off the swing. Or, we would take her out of the high chair and put her in the bath. Her 18-month-old neocortex did not have the capacity to adjust to such a quick micro-transition. Using the Third Space was a godsend in managing her behaviour. The key steps were to give her plenty of notice before the next transition and to paint the next space as amazing and exciting, so she actually looked forward to it. 'We're going to go home and see Mummy. Mummy has Elmo with her. You can sing songs with Mummy and Elmo. Which song will you sing first, Baa Baa or Row Row?'

Setting yourself up well for each micro-transition is the key to reclaiming control of your life.

I was conducting a full day training session on the Third Space with the senior leadership team of a large corporation. During the afternoon tea break, a woman in the group came up to me and said, 'I have just had an "aha!" moment. Last week I went to collect my son from child care when I witnessed him holding down another boy and hitting him repeatedly. What was most concerning was the ferocity with which he was hitting him. At a meeting with the care workers they pointed out that over the last month he had become much more frustrated and angry. While sitting in your workshop, I realised I know what is driving it.'

'What do you think it is?' I asked her.

'I recently received a promotion and my work load has jumped significantly. Between that and being a single mother, time is really scarce. I feel that I'm always behind and as a result, sprint from one thing to another. What I have realised is that my transitions with him are terribly frantic. When I get him up in the morning I am in a flurry to get him out the door on time. Every morning I yell at him to hurry up and get things done. I literally throw him in the door at child care and rush off to work. Then in the afternoon, I'm always running late to pick him up. Once there, I rush him out the door, telling him to "hurry up". At home, it's an absolute sprint to get him fed, washed and in bed. I just realised that I yell at him and rush him through every transition we make throughout the day.' At the close of the workshop, we sat down and came up with some specific strategies she could implement to make his transitions more relaxing and less jarring. Months later, I heard from her that these new strategies resulted in a much calmer and relaxed little boy. She also commented that having to slow down and be more patient in these transitions with her son led to her being more relaxed.

A SELFISH NEED

When I was at university the running joke about psychologists was that they studied psychology in order to sort out their own issues. Like them, my pursuit of the Third Space is partly a selfish one. As a professional presenter I can't have a bad day. I am 'on' all the time. I can't just show up to a presentation and say, 'I'm just going to take it easy today. I'm not in the mood.' The reason I have to be 'on' is that presenting is the only job in which people watch you work, judge you, critique you and hand you an evaluation form at the end of it. Accountants, for example, don't have a group of people standing behind them watching them work, saying, 'Oh I wouldn't have balanced it like that ... gee that's not good. Mmm, I don't agree with that ... Here is your evaluation form!'

I once finished presenting at a conference when the MC jumped up and said, 'Now it's time to rate the speaker. Question number one: 'Did you like the speaker?' Not 'Did you get good value?' or 'Did you find it practical?', but 'Did you like the guy?' Unfortunately for me, the audience had electronic keypads and they could vote in real time. They showed the live results on the screen, so as I was walking off stage I was also finding out what the audience thought of me. I wanted to go home, draw the curtains, turn off the lights and assume the foetal position in the corner. The biggest challenge in this job is not letting things affect your mindset before you go on stage.

PERSONAL LOSS

On two occasions, I experienced devastating personal tragedies right before a presentation, which cemented my need for the Third Space in order to keep doing my job. The first occurred just before I went on stage to present to 5000 people at the Darling Harbour Convention Centre in Sydney. Presenting to an audience that big is all about energy management. A group of 5000 is like a huge ecosystem and in order to keep it alive, you have to feed it. Most importantly, you have to stay in control of it. When that many people laugh it's like a wave that comes at you. You have to ride that wave and drive the energy into your next moment to keep them engaged and focused. When you lose 5000 people you never get them back. Needless to say, I had to 'show up' that day. My normal preparation involves me turning off my phone one hour before my presentation, however on this day I still had my phone on. It rang in my pocket, and as I pulled it out I saw it was my friend Denis, who I think the world of but who isn't the sort of friend who calls. The moment I heard Denis's voice, I knew something was wrong. I asked what was up. Like a baseball bat to the head his words came at me. 'Mark's dead.'

Mark was one of my best mates. We had been practically inseparable since we were 18. When I lived in the US for a stint, I would call home and he would answer the phone. I asked what he was doing at my house. 'Oh, I just came over to have dinner with your folks.' His dad once threatened to charge me rent because I was at his house so often. In fact, I tried to claim ownership of their lounge because I argued that I spent more time on it than they did. I loved him and his family deeply.

Shock and disbelief welled up within me. I thought I was going to throw up, but found myself pacing back and forth, thoughts racing at a million miles an hour. How could he be gone? It's not fair. Holy shit, how is his family feeling right now? This has to be some sort of mistake. For a moment I was lost. I forgot where

I was and what was waiting for me through those doors. How the hell could I present to a group of people now? At this point I had a very big decision to make: do I stay or do I go?

I had to get a serious grip, pull it together. There was nothing I could do for Mark in that moment. His family didn't need to hear from me right then. There was nothing I could do for him or his family. Next door, 5000 people were waiting for me. I slowed down my breathing. I focused on what I wanted to share with the group and why it was important for them to hear it. I ran it over and over in my head. Every time Mark flashed into my head, I tried to block him out. The strange thing was that I ended up giving one of the best presentations I have ever given. I was focused, present and in the zone. It was only once I was off the stage, on my way home, that I fell apart.

The second experience happened a month later.

Over our European holiday my wife and I decided we should start trying to have our first child. When we arrived home, Chris noticed some significant changes in how she felt. The following day we went to the doctor and received the good news: we were expecting our first child. We were elated to say the least, and at the 12-week mark we filled our friends and family in on this new chapter of our life. The following Monday I had to fly to Brisbane to present at the Brisbane Convention Centre to 2500 people. Before I left that morning, Chris complained of stomach pains. The pains were not severe so we decided that I should still go to Brisbane and Chris would go to the doctor. I called her when I landed and she was waiting for her check-up. An hour later I hadn't heard from her. Another hour later, still no word. I'd been calling her frantically but each time it went to voicemail. I had 15 minutes before I was on stage. Then it hit me. Chris had not called or picked up because she had lost the baby. I felt a great despair that I'd never experienced before, as though someone was sitting on my chest. Once again, I had a difficult choice: do I present now, or run home to Chris? In that moment I realised that I could not change this awful situation. I would not be able to get an earlier flight to see her. Once again, I realised these people were counting on me. Considering the situation, my presentation went remarkably well. When I got off stage I sent Chris a message saying, 'I've finished presenting. I need to talk to you right now.' She called me back and confirmed my fears.

What allowed me to perform well in such a state of personal tragedy? It was using the Third Space between receiving the devastating news and walking out on stage. I handled the transitional space, I managed the gap. While both these examples are very emotional and devastating, there would be days where I heard bad news about my business, where I may have had a disagreement with my kids or with Chris, and then I'd have to get up on stage and present. Or there would be days where I lacked confidence and doubted my ability. I realised that if I wanted to continue presenting as much as I did, I had two paths ahead of me: learn how to master my micro-transitions and show up at my best, or face burnout and spend my days in a padded room wearing a jacket that ties up in the back.

DIFFERENT SPACES, DIFFERENT MINDSETS

Quite often, the spaces we transition between require very different and specific mindsets. Work has a very different mindset to home; an internal meeting has a very different mindset to a meeting with a client; doing tasks at your desk requires a very different mindset to leading and interacting with your team; the mindset you need when greeting a client is very different to the mindset needed to do administration work.

My research shows that we are struggling with micro-transitions. I see people who have a disagreement with a co-worker and can't stop thinking about it for days, which kills their productivity. I see managers who have had a frustrating morning at home with the family and take that out on their team at work. In fact, I do a lot of work in the law profession because their leaders struggle to transition from the critical thinkers they need to be as a lawyer, to then being an inspiring and thoughtful leader who engages and leads their team.

When my wife had our first child, her so-called 'baby brain' kicked in big time. She would often use the dog's name when she meant me and vice versa. I remember one day, she stood in our bedroom holding a coathanger, saying to me, 'I need you to take this thing with you.'

'What thing?' I asked.

'This thing!' she replied, shaking the coathanger. 'I want to say umbrella, but I know that's wrong.' I talked to one woman who told me she had placed her baby in the car's baby capsule. The baby was asleep so she placed the capsule on the bottom shelf of her shopping trolley, did her shopping, packed the car, returned the trolley, drove home and sat down for a nice cup of tea. All of a sudden she had a sense that she had forgotten something – her baby. She returned to the shopping centre to find her baby still underneath the trolley, sound asleep.

Is there such a thing as baby brain? Memory issues aren't only experienced by new mothers. Often, women in their 40s and 50s complain of forgetfulness. Men's response to this can sometimes be a terribly patronising: 'They must be hormonal.' Peter M. Meyer, a biostatistician at Chicago's Rush University Medical Center, investigated if hormonal changes disrupt a woman's memory. What he found was that their mind and memory were completely intact. In fact, they were sharp as a tack. What was the problem? Meyer concluded that the cause was in fact 'role overload'. These women had to move between so many roles with competing demands that they spent their day multi-tasking between them. Their brain simply gets overwhelmed.

When I was in the United States attending a conference, I was discussing the concept of multiple roles with a psychologist who told me about a study that showed that the average woman spends 117 hours a week in some sort of role that involves attending to other people. These people might be their partner, their child, someone at work or someone in the community. There are only 168 hours in a week. That leaves 51 hours a week where they are not in some sort of role. That's 7.3 hours per day, during which they need to sleep, wash themselves and go to the bathroom.

WHY DO WE STRUGGLE WITH MICRO-TRANSITIONS?

There are two reasons we struggle with micro-transitions. Firstly, we lack the behavioural flexibility to alter our mindset and behaviour to suit the next space we move into. The challenge is *showing up* with the right mindset for that new space and leaving the baggage – if you have any – of the previous space behind you. This skill allows a surgeon to show up engaged and focused for surgery, when that morning she has found out that her daughter is in trouble at school for using drugs. This skill allows a manager to motivate his team after he has been yelled at by the general manager for poor performance.

Secondly, we have a huge lack of awareness of the micro-transitions we make. When I interviewed the people included in this book about how they handle their challenging micro-transitions, many of them said, 'Um ... can I have time to think about that?'

How do we handle our micro-transitions better? It all comes down to becoming conscious of what we do or don't do in the Third Space. When we pay little attention to the Third Space we 'show up' unprepared, simply reacting to the environment, haunted by the thoughts and emotions of the space we just left. Using the Third Space effectively means you choose how you 'show up'. It's about rapidly changing mindsets to get your head in the game – fast!

Over the years, a couple of people have asked me, 'This Third Space, isn't it teaching us to be disingenuous and act like different people all the time?' Nothing could be further from the truth. It's not about putting on a different face or becoming a different person. Rather, it is about understanding the different subtleties of the various spaces we move between throughout our day and then altering our behaviour to suit them.

At its simplest level, the objective of the Third Space is to show up with the right emotions, thoughts and behaviour to effectively transition into the Second Space. Behaviour comprises our posture, presence, energy levels, facial expressions, choice of words and tone of voice.

How we perform in the Second Space is a result of the thoughts, emotions and behaviour we bring into it. These determine our success and the quality of the interactions we have. This is the *essence* of the Third Space. From Chapter 5 ('Check your baggage at the door'), we will dive deep into the Third Space and dissect transitions into a step-by-step process that will help you transition effectively in each area of your life. But before we enter this little rabbit hole we call the Third Space, let's stay on the surface to help you understand why this concept is so valuable to your life.

Each space requires its own unique blend of thoughts, emotions and behaviour. For example, a boxer stepping in the ring for a fight needs the following:

Thoughts – 'I am untouchable. This fight is mine. I have trained hard and I'm in the best shape of my life.'

Emotions – enthusiasm, aggression, zest, optimism, nervousness.

Behaviour – energetic: bouncing around, confident, imposing, strong posture, staring his opponent down.

If he shows up with the following, he's dead meat:

Thoughts – 'I'm not sure if I am ready for this, I hope I don't get hurt, my preparation has not been as good as it could have been.'

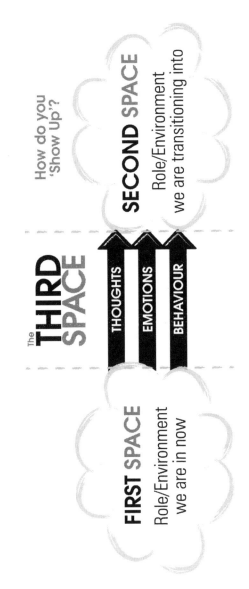

Emotions – fear, panic, uncertainty.

Behaviour – slumped shoulders, avoiding eye contact, moving sluggishly.

Now imagine a manager whose direct report is stressed and struggling with their workload. The manager needs to show up in the following way:

Thoughts – 'So-and-so is a great team member; I need to let them voice their issues and not judge them on that. I need to not take anything they say personally, take my ego out of it and just focus on a resolution. I've been in their situation in the past myself. Everyone has a bad day.'

Emotions – empathy, compassion, patience, affection, friendliness.

Behaviour – relaxed posture, gentle, being present, calm, soft vocal tone, active listening.

How they do not want to show up is like this:

Thoughts – 'I am sick to death of their crap, would they just get it together, I have so much to do I do not have time for this.'

Emotions – frustration, annoyance, anger.

Behaviour – stiff posture, finishing their sentences for them, huffing.

Even as parents, we need to be aware of how we are 'showing up'. For example, your child wants to tell you about his or her day at preschool while you're preparing dinner:

Thoughts – 'It's important that I pay attention and let them tell me about their day. This will help them grow to enjoy and like school more. They will be in bed soon and I won't get to see them again until tomorrow. I love it when they tell me about their day and it is so cute when they go off on tangents and get confused.'

Emotions – love, excitement, enthusiasm.

Behaviour – being present by coming down to their level, looking them in the eye, asking questions, smiling.

What you don't want is this:

Thoughts – 'I can never get a moment to myself. Gee, kid, just get to the point. I need to get dinner on as fast as possible. This task is more important than listening to you waffle on.'

Emotions – annoyance, contempt.

Behaviour – not listening, no eye contact, focusing on the other task.

SELF-AWARENESS AND PERSONAL RESPONSIBILITY

The Third Space facilitates you to be aware of your behaviour and take personal responsibility for how you transition and 'show up'. The reality is that all we have any control over are the thoughts we think, the emotions we feel and the behaviour we exhibit. We don't control other people, we don't control our partner, we don't control the economy and we don't control the fact that some of the people we work with have been taking pain-in-the-arse pills for the last five years.

I have the amazing pleasure of getting to work with thousands of people each year. I get to visit many organisations, some of which are performing really well and some of which are incredibly dysfunctional. Within those organisations I meet people who are high performers as well as those whom the organisation would like to see walk out the door and never return. What is glaringly obvious is that the difference between these groups of people is their ability to be aware of their behaviour and take personal responsibility for altering it as need be. The Third Space facilitates both of these.

THE THIRD SPACE IS PRACTICAL

When I was developing this concept, I presented it to a group of academic psychologists for feedback. What they loved about the idea was that it gave people a practical framework in which to introduce self-awareness and behaviour modification into their day. They said, 'Psychology today is coming up with amazing developments and new tools for people to improve their wellbeing. However, the challenge is finding a way to get them to practically introduce these techniques into their day. The Third Space inserts these latest theories into something that we all do day in and day out. It's not like meditation where you have to take 30 minutes out of your day to do it. We are presented with the Third Space multiple times in our day. It's a matter of slotting these techniques into a part of our life that already exists.'

They are right, though. We don't have an information problem, we have an implementation problem. The real challenge is changing behaviour. Using the Third Space does not require countless hours put aside to practise it. You can use this technique in real time, and the great news is that if you screw up one micro-transition, you simply have to wait for the next one before you have another go. This, I believe, is the real value of the technique.

The Third Space is simply the gap in which you shut down the first space and prepare yourself to be at your best for the Second Space. Start to think counter-intuitively about transitions – three comes before two.

Now, it is all well and good to tell you to 'show up' better. It's like the motivational speaker who tells you to 'be positive'. The problem with this message is that it's too vague. People need a process to change their behaviour, and they need a framework. From Chapter 5 onwards, we will unpack a four-phase model around effective micro-transitions.

However, before we do that we need to ground this concept in reality by exploring a micro-transition that we can all relate to. The next chapter will explore the micro-transition we seem to struggle with the most: the micro-transition from work to home.

SUMMARY

- The world is so fast-paced that the time we get in each space is being compressed. The result is that our lives are boiled down to a series of small spaces.
- The key to a happy, fulfilled life is the ability to embrace and get the most out of each space. Utilising the Third Space ensures this happens.

- Each space we move into has a very different and specific mindset. We need to 'show up' with a mindset that suits each new space. This improves our performance, our relationships and our happiness.

- At its basic level, the Third Space allows us to 'show up' with the right thoughts, emotions and behaviour for the next space. It develops our self-awareness and leads us to take personal responsibility for our behaviour.

Chapter 3

I'm coming home!

In the early 1950s, women were given 'wife manuals'. Yes, they're as bad as they sound. It was literally a manual on how to be a good wife. One of the things the manual focused on was how a wife should treat her 'man' when he came home from work. They were instructed to let their husbands unload for ten to 15 minutes as they may have had a busy day. The wife's role was to help her husband get his day off his chest and unwind.

Can you believe this was only about 60 years ago? But (and stay with me here) while this is incredibly misogynistic, we can learn from the basic premise. My research shows that the micro-transition between work and home has a significant impact on our lives. Unfortunately it is a micro-transition that we constantly struggle with. The Third Space that exists between work and home may be the most important transition of your day.

TRANSITIONING FROM PSYCHO BUSINESSMAN TO SUPER DAD

My company runs a healthcare business called The Glucose Club, which helps people alter their lifestyle in terms of how physically active they are, what they eat and how they approach the psychology of change. The goal of this business is to improve our clients' health, quality of life and well-being, as well as lessening their chance of developing chronic diseases such as obesity, diabetes and heart disease. In 2002 a high-profile Australian businessman joined The Glucose Club. He was someone who clearly had a lot going on in his life and certainly had a high degree of stress. We had our first meeting in his home at 7.30pm, in order to understand his home environment. While we were talking about his lifestyle something stood out about him: he was incredibly relaxed, calm, engaged, fun, present and energetic with his family.

I thought, 'That's how I want to be when I get home.'

Once we finished the session I said, 'I hope this question isn't out of line, but how do you go from "psycho businessman" to "super dad"?'

'Well, I used to get it very wrong,' he replied. 'Previously, I would walk in the door, finishing my wife's sentences because she doesn't talk fast enough. I was yelling at my kids because they weren't efficient with the time they had available to them. In effect I was trying to run my home like I ran my office. It got to the point where I came home one day and as I opened the door the kids scattered. They literally ran away from me when they heard me coming home. It broke my heart. What sort of a jerk comes home and their kids don't even want to see them? I realised that I was this hurricane that tore through the house and left a trail of destruction behind me. Desperate times called for desperate measures.'

At this point his teenage son came home. After the introduction, he asked what we were doing. His father replied, 'I'm filling Adam in on "cave time".'

'We love cave time,' I heard the son mutter as he walked off. What the heck was 'cave time'?

He continued. 'After finding out that the kids dreaded me walking through the door, I built a new entrance into the house.' (I realise many of you might not have the cash flow to do this but read on.)

'You did what?'

'Let me show you,' he said. The businessman then walked me into the garage. 'See that doorway? That leads straight to my bedroom. I park the car, get out, go through the doorway and straight into my room without talking to anyone in the family. The first thing I do is have a shower. I get dressed in casual clothes, and then I do a relaxation exercise that lasts for about two minutes. After that, I go out to greet the family.

'I lose 15 to 20 minutes but the mindset I'm in is worth every minute. In that time I think about how I want to be when I go out to greet the family: how I want to act, how I want to feel, and how I want to make them feel. In the house we call it "cave time". In fact, one of the house rules is: don't interrupt Dad during cave time.'

'How does your wife feel about you not interacting with her when you come home?' I asked.

'Ask her yourself.'

When we quizzed his wife, she told us. 'You know what? I can forgive long hours and I can forgive him loving his work. What I can't forgive is him walking through that door and taking his day out on us or not giving us the attention we deserve. When he comes home I need him to stop being the businessman and be my partner and a father to the kids. But at the same time I have to be empathetic to him and understand that he needs time to unwind after the day. Giving him that time is one of the most significant things we've done in our 30 years of marriage. I just wish we'd done it earlier.'

This was it. This was the Third Space in action. I started to include this story and the concept in my presentations. The response was amazing. People immediately resonated with this concept of having a Third Space between work and home. It was great for business, too, because so many women came up to me and said, 'Could you go present to my husband's company? I want him to transition home better.' I received hundreds of emails from people informing me of their new-found Third Space, describing what a huge impact it had made on their life and relationships. These ranged from going to the gym or walking the dog, to walking home. An elderly gentleman in one of my sessions told me about how he grew up in a country town where all the men would go to the pub after work and have a couple of drinks before it closed at 6pm. He said that at the pub you would have a whinge to your mates about the day and a few laughs that would put you in a good mood to go home. Not that I'm saying that you need to call into the local on your way home. But still, this is a Third Space.

IT WORKED FOR ME

I tried it myself. I come home from two environments – either from the office, which is located in a separate building on my property, or the airport. When I am coming home from the airport I park my car there so I can drive home rather than get a cab. I find sharing that trip home with a cab driver is not conducive to me unwinding. When I drive home I play the Best of Queen album loudly and sing at the top of my voice (don't judge me). When I come in, I go straight upstairs to my room, get out of my suit and then go to greet my family.

When I'm in the office my Third Space revolves around my dog Tilly. Tilly is a blue English Staffordshire Bull Terrier. She is 18 kilograms of pure enthusiasm and love. I finish work at 4.30pm and take her for a one-hour walk. It's brilliant – fresh air, exercise and spending time with someone that loves you more than life. Our most recent addition to the family, my daughter Isabella, usually joins us for this walk. It's great to have one-on-one time with her and it also gives my wife some much needed alone time where she can relax or get things done. Everyone wins. The dog is worn out, Bells has a run around in the park and I've forgotten about work.

I found this technique invaluable and I saw a dramatic improvement in my behaviour at home following the Third Space. In fact, everyone I knew who implemented this strategy got results.

Why does this resonate with people so well? The reason is that people feel the pain of transitioning poorly from work to home. At work, the mindset is one that revolves around efficiency, quick decisions, navigating the political landscape, beating the competition and the completion of tasks. However, if you take this mindset home it will certainly lead to conflict.

WORK-LIFE BALANCE

One phrase that people kept associating the Third Space with was 'work-life balance'. They often said that when they implemented this technique they felt that they experienced greater balance. Work-life balance is an interesting area – in the corporate world it seems that people have fallen out of love with this term. The challenge with balance is that it is a subjective term. One person's view of balance is quite different to another. While many people may argue and debate the term work-life balance, we seem to be stuck with it simply because we understand it and everyone uses it.

With many of the companies I work with we use an online stress diagnostic tool called 'The Redline Program'. This program is unique in that it categorises your stress into three types – Physical, Emotional or Intellectual. The test identifies the key drivers of stress in your life. Regardless of which industry we use this tool with, whether it is with coal miners or investment bankers, lack of work-life balance is one of the top three drivers of stress. Most people find it difficult to keep their work and personal life balanced.

One day, a friend of mine said something that made me choke on my coffee. He said, 'For the first 12 months of my daughter's life I did not see her awake.' I challenged this immediately.

'You cannot be serious.'

'I am deadly serious.'

'What the hell were you doing?'

'I was the managing partner of a law firm.'

Enough said. Clearly this is an example of work-life balance out of control.

The main thing we know about balance is that most people aren't happy with their level of it. Our level of work-life balance in Australia does not paint a pretty picture. Sixty per cent of women and almost half of men feel constantly time-pressured to successfully juggle home and work. The majority of working Australians thought that long working hours has negative effects on the rest of life, creating strain and restricting time they have to themselves, families, friends and communities.[1]

There are differing theories surrounding work-life balance and people argue their views with a tremendous amount of passion. After wading through the research, it became so complicated that I needed pain medication and a lie-down. However, we must remember that this formal research has its limitations. Many university studies use a population made up of undergraduate and MBA students which gives us a skewed view on balance because it often samples from the same group. (When I was a student, the only thing I worried about in terms of balance was, 'Should I go to the uni bar now or later?') I paired this research with the surveys we completed in corporations as well as the thousands of conversations that I had with people I met while speaking at conferences. When I put it all together I saw some very distinct patterns. First of all let's look at where we go wrong with balance.

COMMON WORK-LIFE BALANCE MISTAKES

LISTENING TO OTHERS

We forget that balance is personal. What may be balance for you is certainly not balance for others. In addition, balance is something that is greatly influenced by a person's stage of life. A single person's view of balance was very different to someone with a partner and kids. Likewise, a person who was responsible for the care of elderly parents also saw balance in a very different light. One consistent theme that I observed was that people felt very much judged when it came to balance. They felt that other people imposed their views of balance on them. In particular, working mothers felt hugely judged and persecuted regarding balance. The people who felt happiest with their level of balance marched to their own beat. They assessed what worked for them and applied their own theory around balance.

Determine your own path and don't bow to what people think you should do to achieve balance.

WAITING FOR IT TO ARRIVE

Many people expect to just get it. Balance is not something that creeps up behind you and jumps on your back so you then have it for life, like herpes or luggage. Our lives are constantly in a state of flux. Sometimes we need to focus more on home, other times we need to spend more time at work. Balance is something that we will always be juggling with and something that we must review and check often.

OUTSOURCING THE RESPONSIBILITY TO OTHERS

I frequently talk to people who think it is the responsibility of their workplace to give them balance. While it would be great to work for a company that helps us with balance (personally, I think it is in the company's interest to support and facilitate balance), the reality is often different. Companies are set up to make money and the more work they can squeeze out of you the more money they make. This is the harsh reality of the corporate world. Don't outsource your work-life balance to your company because they may not be coming to the rescue.

SO HOW DO WE ACHIEVE BALANCE?

1. CREATE BOUNDARIES

One theory within work-life balance is called the boundary theory. It is as it sounds – develop clear boundaries between work and home.

People with weak boundaries between work and home have been shown to experience more conflict between the those two worlds, while clear boundaries have been shown to reduce work-family conflict, leading to greater work-family harmony.[2] People who achieve greater work-family harmony exhibit better physical health, less stress and improved job performance and satisfaction than those who do not achieve it.[3]

Recently, organisations have woken up to the importance of balance for their employees, especially for the new generation entering the workforce.

Universum is a US company that specialises in employer branding to help companies attract the best and the brightest. It conducts an annual survey of over 300,000 students and 80,000 professionals in 20 countries and regularly reports that work-life balance is often the number one career goal of students above all else, including remuneration.

Clearly a lack of balance is an issue for people at all stages of life. In response to this, organisations are trying to brand themselves as supporters of work-life balance to attract more talented employees. They see facilitating balance as:

- flexible work hours
- working from home
- job-sharing
- family leave programs (parental leave, compassionate leave, paternal leave)
- on-site child care
- on-site gyms or corporate health programs.

Are these strategies improving our level of balance?

Researchers suggest that some of these strategies blur the lines between home and work, and that many organisations 'weaken these boundaries through "progressive" work features, such as on-site day care centres and gyms which allow employees' personal lives to enter the workplace,' and 'alternative work arrangements, such as telework, flexible work options and technology (internet, laptops and smartphones) that allow work to enter the non-work sphere'.[4] The blurring of these lines made some people feel like they were 'on' all the time and could not differentiate between work and personal time.

But is the blurring of these lines necessarily a bad thing? Do we need to be black and white to get balance? Many people I spoke to said that this blurring of boundaries actually improved their balance. Some said that they checked emails and did work at 9pm. While that sounds like a complete lack of balance, doing this allows them to come home at 6pm and be with their family while the kids are awake. When the kids go to bed, they're able to do work. While they said it was not ideal, the alternative was to stay at work until 7.30pm and miss seeing the kids altogether. Likewise, one manager said that she was at her boys' school sports carnival and took a phone call on her mobile from the office. One of the other mums gave her a hard time, saying, 'Why don't you turn your phone off and pay attention to your kid?'

The manager pointed out to the other mum that the phone allowed her to be there for her sons. The alternative was to stay at work and miss the carnival altogether. Many people interviewed also said that on-site gyms or day care centres allowed them to save a tremendous amount of time that they could then dedicate to other things.

Once again, we have to exercise our own judgement and determine if the blurring of boundaries is helping our balance or killing it. For me, personally, I rarely do work after I enter the home environment. The phone and computer are checked at the door. However, while writing this book I often had to start writing again after 8pm. While this was not ideal, I did not feel it killed my balance as I'd already had two to three hours of quality interaction with my family.

Having clear boundaries between work and home would be ideal, but the reality may be different. We have to be aware that those two worlds co-exist and we need to be constantly vigilant in not letting one have a detrimental impact on the other for too long. The reality is that home is more flexible and forgiving than work and, as such, is often the one that suffers when work puts the squeeze on us.

If you have a job that is contained to a specific workplace such as machine operator or production line worker, it's obviously easier to separate work and home. However, with the reduction of these roles, longer working hours and development of technology, it is harder to draw a clear barrier between work and home. If you run your own business, or if you are a medical practitioner, teacher or corporate employee, the worlds of work and home often collide.

Key drivers of work-family conflict are:
- bringing physical work home with you
- contact with work colleagues at home
- work-family multi-tasking (such as checking email at the dinner table).

2. CREATE MENTAL BOUNDARIES

Rather than focus on pushing back on the world, let's shift our focus to changing behaviour. We may not be able to clearly separate work and home on a physical level but we can all do it on a mental level.

When we interview participants in our programs who complain about their balance, we ask them, 'What would balance look like?' The most common response revolves around the metric of time. They say, 'Balance would mean I would have more time with my friends and family.' In my experience, time is the wrong metric for balance. If balance isn't about time what is it about? I don't think we want balance! There, I said it. What we really want is to be happy and have fulfilling relationships. Saying you want balance is like saying you want to be on a diet. You don't want to be on a diet, what you really want is to be thinner. The diet is the vehicle to get you to be thinner. Likewise, balance is the vehicle to happiness and positive relationships. The problem is that we focus on the vehicle, not the outcome. I have friends who claim to have great balance because they are home a lot. However, the only time they interact with their family is to grunt at them if they get in the way of the TV. Rather than focus on how much time we spend in each part of our lives, I believe we need to focus instead on the *quality* of this time.

When I interview people on whether their partner exhibited balance at the end of the day, the single biggest complaint I hear is that while their partner was physically at home, their attention was somewhere else. Put simply, they were not present in the home environment. They were either interacting with some sort of medium (TV, computer, reading material) or thinking about other things. Our mind is continuously bouncing around. This is a barrier to balance. It is often said that the greatest compliment we can give a human being is our undivided attention, yet we rarely do it. If we are never truly present at any moment how can we invest in and improve our relationships and ourselves? Isn't that what balance is all about? Being present creates a mental boundary between home and work. So while you might need to do some work at home, when you have interactions with your family, aim to be completely present with them, rather than splitting your attention two ways.

In our research, when we asked people to practise being present in the home environment they felt that their level of balance had improved. Best of all, their family and friends also believed that they were doing a better job of being balanced. Work-life balance is more than creating a physical barrier between work and home. You also need a mental barrier where you can say, 'I am in home mode now and I will be present and engaged in this new environment'. Likewise, when you enter work, you need a mental barrier so that you can now focus and be present at work.

3. REDUCE NEGATIVE SPILL

There is strong evidence to show that stress in one domain – work – transfers and has a negative impact on the other domain – home.[5] In fact, work-family conflict reduces a person's job-life satisfaction. The problem is that many people transfer stress from one part of their lives to the next. Often, we take work stress home with us. It comes home in the form of frustration, tiredness and anger. When we enter the home space like this it leads to conflict. A snappy comment or passive aggressive behaviour leads to poor home interactions which in turn creates more stress. If we live on our own, work baggage can lead to us ruminating about the day and stop us from going out and socialising. We then take this stress to work with us the next day. Once again, it leads to conflict at work, leading to further stress. The cycle continues and our stress levels continue to build.

Tim Gard is a US-based speaker and friend of mine who teaches organisations to recognise the value of using humour in the workplace. He talks about how we finish our work day and we grab a bag. In that bag we put all the negative events that have happened to us that day: 'Here's the fact that I'm taken for granted at work; here's the fact that I don't have the right resources to do my job and my staff are lazy.' It all goes in the bag. Then we say to the people we work with, 'See you tomorrow, I'm going home,' and we take that bag home. We walk in the door and the people we live with ask us how our day was. We reply, 'How was my day? How was my day? Here's my day (as we slam the bag down in front of them). How would you like that day? How do you think I feel after that day?' This leads to conflict in the home, which results in an increase in stress. The result is more stuff to put in the bag. 'Here's the fact that my partner is distant and critical, here's the fact that my kids are selfish and don't think about my needs.' It all goes in the bag and we say to our family, 'See ya, I'm going to work.' The cycle continues.

An essential part of having balance is the ability to not carry the negative baggage from one space in your life to the next. I refer to this as negative spill. You don't want to carry the negative spill from each space of your life to the next one.

A vital aspect to balance is having a circuit-breaker between home and work, and then between work and home. A place you can put all that negative stuff in a bag, but you put it down, turn to it and say, 'Stay.' You walk away and are able to show up at home or work clean.

The key to balance is to minimise the negative impact that work has on your personal life and the negative impact that personal life has on work. The Third Space is where you dump your negative baggage.

4. MAXIMISE POSITIVE SPILL

If there's anything you want to carry over from work or home it's the positive things. I call this positive spill. When we carry positive experiences from work into the home environment, it leads to better behaviour at home. All too often, as we go home we think of the bad things that happened during the day and what we forgot to do or what we didn't get right. If we bring home the good experiences of the day, our mood and interactions will greatly improve. We will specifically look at how to do this later in the book.

To improve balance, we want a circuit-breaker between work and home and again between home and work. We want this circuit-breaker to do four things:

- Help us be present in the new environment we are in.
- Minimise negative spill from the previous space.
- Maximise positive spill from the previous space.
- Create a physical or mental barrier.

WHY WE NEED THE THIRD SPACE BETWEEN WORK AND HOME

If you transition into your home with negative thoughts, emotions and behaviour, what sort of an evening are you setting yourself up for? How you 'show up' sets the tone for the interaction you have with yourself or the people in your home. You don't necessarily have to have a family to improve how you 'show up' at home. If you live on your own, the work-to-home Third Space is important in order to turn off from the day and show up in a more relaxed and composed mindset when you arrive home. This will make it easier to reduce stress, focus on the things you want to do when you get home or connect with friends. Unfortunately, the average person is not doing this. In fact, we have found that they are 'showing up' poorly.

We surveyed 831 people, all professionals from various industries, and got them to note down what thoughts, emotions and behaviour they presented when they transitioned into their homes at the end of the day. Of the 831 people, 613 completed the survey, and 73 per cent had responses that we classified as negative.

THOUGHTS

We found that the most common thoughts were incredibly negative:

'I have had a tough day, I'm not in the mood to deal with my kids and they are driving me crazy.'

'I just know what she (my wife) is going to say to me when I get in the door. "Why are you late again?" I'm late because my manager is an idiot who gives me extra work to do as I am heading out the door. She has it so easy compared to me. She gets to stay home while I have to go out and work my arse off. Just once, I would like her to appreciate me for how hard I work.'

'For God's sake, does it ever end? I never seem to get a chance to catch my breath. It's just go, go, go. I work really hard during the day only to come home to cook dinner, and clean up after my roommates. Then on top of that I have to do emails. I just feel like I never get time to even scratch myself.'

'It's so depressing to come home to an empty house. It feels like I have no life. I haven't had a relationship in seven months and my friends are distant. All I seem to do is work and sleep. I want to meet someone but I just don't have the energy to get out.'

'I feel like I'm drowning. It feels like my life is out of control; there are never enough hours to get everything done. I am so disorganised. Between the family and study I don't have a moment of calm.'

EMOTIONS

We also found that the most common emotions were mostly negative:

- fatigue
- frustration
- anger
- despair
- sadness
- relief
- resentment
- stress (not really an emotion, more of a state or symptom).

BEHAVIOUR

Some respondents said that they deliberately baited their partner to start a fight. They were hypercritical of their partner, not present and uninterested. Many said they were so tired they had no enthusiasm to do anything.

'Felt anxious and stressed, found it hard to sleep. Hyper, fidgety and I appear quite manic and disorganised.'

'Tense, angry, all worked up, just looked at my posture – it looks like I am about to go into battle. I must look very aggressive to other people.'

On the positive side, approximately 27 per cent of respondents 'showed up' at home with the following:

Thoughts – 'I can't wait to see my family. I'm really grateful for the people in my life.' 'I'm looking forward to relaxing when I get home and reading my book.'

Emotions – gratitude, love, tolerance, empathy, calmness.

Behaviour – being able to turn off and be present, calm, relaxed, welcoming, fun, energised.

Read on to find out how others use the Third Space between work and home to 'show up' better.

SUMMARY

We struggle to effectively transition between work and home. We often bring the stress of the day home with us or take the stress of home to work. The result is that we are not present or engaged in either environment.

The majority of people are not happy with their level of balance.

The top three mistakes around balance are:

1. Listening to the opinions and expectations of others.
2. Waiting for it to magically happen.
3. Expecting others to give it to you.

To achieve balance we:

- ideally have physical boundaries between work and home
- create a mental boundary between work and home and practise being present
- minimise negative spill from the previous environment
- maximise positive spill from the previous environment.

Chapter 4

Do as they do

Using the Third Space between work and home is where you apply the principles of 'showing up'. Ask yourself what your current thoughts, emotions and behaviour are. Will they improve the experience you will have in your home? If the answer is 'no', use the Third Space to change them. Just because your last meeting at work was full of politics and sniping, not to mention out-and-out hostility, it doesn't mean you have to bring that atmosphere into your home environment.

Here are some case studies of people who have improved their balance by using the Third Space between work and home.

I received the following email from Mike Leonard, Manager Information Services at Shellharbour City Council.

At the conference, you told the story about the dad who got home from work and came in through a separate entrance and spent time in his Third Space cooling down and preparing to spend quality time with his family. This resonated with me but with a slight twist. My partner and I work together, and even worse I am her direct manager. Yeah, yeah I know ... I deserve a medal or a lead tablet (maybe both). We worked together for a long time as colleagues and had a great, but only friendly, relationship. Over years this changed and eventually we became partners.

When we first moved in together, we went through a few rough years where we constantly seemed to be spending our personal time together discussing, debating, rehashing and often fighting over situations and events at work. It caused us many problems and it eventually seemed like we were always at work because it pervaded every part of our life together. This had not been a problem before because we went to separate homes after work and had time to 'defuse' (our 'Third Space'). Also, before we lived together we spent much less personal time together so it was precious and we rarely discussed work except in the work environment.

We eventually came up with what we saw as a workable arrangement and agreed never to talk about work-related issues away from the office. This worked for a very short time. Eventually, we would find ourselves sitting together in the lounge room, unable to concentrate on a book or TV show because we were seething about something that happened at work. Alternatively, if I wasn't worried about anything at work I would sit in the lounge room or at the dinner table and wonder what my partner was thinking, sure that she had the dirts with me over some work issue, just because she was a bit quiet. There were unavoidable explosions where the feelings held inside eventually erupted and then they seemed even worse than they had been before.

We decided that we had to do something and that we didn't want to waste precious home time together talking about work stuff. We came up with a brilliant idea. We spend exactly ten minutes together each day in the car travelling home from work. There is a roundabout exactly halfway in the journey. From the time we get in the car to come home, my partner has five minutes to vent and tell me anything she wants about work. What I did wrong, what she did right, who annoyed her that day (mostly me), etc. The rules are I'm not allowed to speak or interrupt her time. Once we get to the roundabout it's my turn. I have five minutes to do the same and she can't interrupt me. Once we hit the driveway at home, work discussions are banned.

Over the first few weeks we became experts at talking really fast. Many people would drive past us, see all the hand waving and gesturing and probably think murder was being committed in the car. The first five minutes at home were still tense but better after that. Then a funny thing happened throughout the following months. The talking be-came slower and the time at home got better. We've been doing this now for about a year. I'm happy to report that the trip home is about one minute of calm explanation, apologies and expectations from my partner, then four minutes of silence to the roundabout. And the pattern repeats for the rest of the trip home when it's my turn.

About two or three weeks ago we actually had a trip home where all that was said was, 'You know how I feel about things today, and I apologise for being short with you.' The reply was, 'Yeah I'm sorry too. I understand how you feel and I'll try harder.' Sometimes the full five minutes is still used, but it's generally a calmer more gentle five minutes.

The twist that I see is this: we still have our 'Third Space' and it serves the same purpose that you described in your talk. But just like the rest of our lives that are so closely shared, so is our 'Third Space'. It works for us. We still have our times apart which are healthy and productive for us. My partner loves to relax and read and I love to tour the back blocks of Australia on my motorbike. We are calmer and more able to accept one another's views and opinions. By the way, communication and situation and relationship management have improved at work, too.

CEO OF A JEWELLERY COMPANY

I was speaking at a CEO networking group where 15 CEOs come together once a month to discuss issues and mentor each other. A woman in the group put up her hand and said, 'I don't have a Third Space, but I do have a Third Person!'

'I don't have a Third Space, but I do have a Third Person!'

Fifteen sets of eyebrows shot up at the same time as we all jumped to the same conclusion.

Everyone held their breath as they waited to see how I would handle the woman's 'confession'. I eventually cleared my throat and said, 'Look, that's great, but it's not that kind of event.'

'No, I'm not having an affair,' she said, bursting out laughing. 'Get your minds out of the gutter! My Third Space is my 10-yearold Down syndrome boy, Blake.

As soon as I get home, Blakey and I colour in together. He tells me about his day, I tell him about my day. That 20 minutes allows me to shift from busy CEO to doting mother and partner.'

When we caught up seven months later she told me that one day a fellow CEO in her group called her and said, 'I have had a really tough day. Do you think I could come over and colour in with you guys?'

One great thing about the Third Space used here is that it involves a task that calms her down, focuses her mind and allows her to connect with her son.

PUMP SOME IRON

A friend of mine went through a divorce and moved out to live on her own. She works in a senior management role and found herself going home to a microwave dinner and half an hour of bad TV and then straight into work. What she found was that she became incredibly stale, lacked energy and seemed to just go through the motions. The big problem was that she fell into the habit of constantly working. There was no down time or time out. When we caught up I told her about the Third Space. She decided to have an extended Third Space every night of the week. Each night of the week, in the transition between work and home, she would do something that did not involve work.

Monday was going to the gym.

Tuesday was Italian classes.

Wednesday was pole dancing classes.

Thursday was gym.

Friday was drinks and dinner after work with a colleague or friend.

The change in her was huge. She felt like she was investing back in herself, she gained more energy and was enjoying life once again. Her mood elevated and she became more enthusiastic at work, which made her more productive and innovative.

COUNSELLOR

I recently presented to a group of counsellors. Let me ask you: what do counsellors do all day? Listen to people's problems. People go to counsellors to unload all their grief, frustration and hurt. No one goes to a counsellor and says, 'Just wanted to let you know that life rocks! Family is great, work's awesome. Just thought you should know.' No, they see a counsellor to talk about what is wrong with their lives and unload their problems.

When a counsellor goes home after work to his or her family, often what do they get? More problems. The burnout rate in counselling is incredibly high because counsellors are constantly looking after the well-being of others and taking on their problems, leaving little for themselves.

After my presentation a woman came up to thank me and said she would go home and try the Third Space. I received an email from her months later saying the Third Space concept had totally changed her life. I asked her specifically what she had done.

'As soon as I get in the door at the end of the day the kids have to go to the rumpus room (their garage has been converted to a play room). They are not allowed out for 30 minutes.' She then said, 'My husband is not allowed home during that time.' When I asked her what she did with those 30 minutes, her reply was, 'Whatever the hell I want! I may have a bath, read a trashy magazine, or have a glass of wine and listen to music. It's the only 30 minutes of the day I have to myself, where I'm not responsible for another human being. One day, I came home and literally stared at the wall for 30 minutes. NO ONE interferes with that time – my kids could be bleeding from the eyes and they would not get my attention during that time.'

I asked how this strategy had affected her life.

'I could not even begin to measure its impact. I'm less stressed, the relationships with my family are better and I am a better counsellor. I love it.' She then went on to say, 'I told my friends I do this and do you know what they called me? They told me I was selfish and a bad mother.'

I asked how she felt about that.

'Screw that!' she said. 'I deserve that time; it's important for me and in fact I am a better mother because of it.'

Let's analyse her example: After this 30-minute break, her thoughts would be more positive, more rational and more accurate. Her emotions would be more positive, calmer and more balanced. Her behaviour would be less stressed, less tense and more at ease.

CAUGHT OUT!

I recently had someone come up to me at a conference who said that his Third Space had almost backfired on him. He said, 'I'm an accountant in a big firm. My job is quite stressful and I find it hard to be engaged with my family. When I get home, my head is still spinning from the day. My wife used to be in a similar occupation and level to me and she is finding it tough being a stay-at-home mum. When I walk in the door, it's like being attacked by a fox terrier: she is at me wanting some adult interaction, wanting me to take care of the kids. She is lovely about it but it doesn't give me a chance to wind down. Unfortunately,

I live quite close to work. It's only an eight-minute drive home, which is not enough time to wind down. I started to drive part of the way home, park my car, recline the seat and to listen to a relaxation CD before I got home. It worked a treat! I was more relaxed, more tolerant and more empathetic to my wife. Unfortunately, one day my wife decided to take the kids for a walk, and happened to walk past my car, which was parked out the front of a strange house. She didn't say a word but was obviously suspicious. The next day she did the same thing only to find my car parked in the same spot. She crept up to my car to peer inside, to find me reclined on the seat. Obviously, there were some questions asked and a heated discussion.

'Initially, she was offended that I wasn't desperately rushing home to see her but after a while saw the value in it. She then agreed for me to have my Third Space in the car in the garage rather than down the street. I still do it to this day.'

WALK THE PAVEMENT

I once worked with a manager of a call centre in Tasmania. Tragically, he had a mild heart attack while I was consulting there. When he came back to work I told him about the concept of the Third Space. I suggested that maybe he could use exercise as his Third Space as it would improve his heart function and also help him wind down after work. Specifically, we came up with a plan for him to do a 30-minute walk as soon as he got home. I ran into him nearly nine months later.

When I asked him how it was going, he said, 'I have not missed a day since you told me to do it'. I was stunned. 'That is amazing; your motivation must be incredible.' He said, 'Oh no, motivation has nothing to do with it. As soon as I get in the door, my wife grabs my bag, hands me the raincoat and says, "On your way."

'Because I'm in such a good mood after my walk, she will not let me miss it. The problem is Tassie in July: it's zero degrees and horizontal rain is hitting me in the face as I open the door, but my wife is pushing me in the back, saying, "You'll be okay. Off you go."'

PARK THE CAR

In a similar vein, a client of mine, Jordan Hawke, Executive General Manager of Asteron Life, saw me present the Third Space concept to his organisation. When he reflected on this concept, he realised that the people at work got the best of him. At work he was energetic, fun, optimistic and engaged. However, when he went home his family got the worst of him. Not that he was openly horrible to them, he just showed up better at work than at home. He gave the best of himself to work. Jordan lives in a gorgeous suburb of Sydney called Manly. Due to his position in the company he has a parking space right under the building. After my presentation he now parks the car outside the city and does a six-kilometre walk into and out of the city. On the way in to work he listens to music on his iPod. He thinks about what is coming up in the day and starts to visualise it – how he wants it to work and what his focus will be. In contrast, on the way home he doesn't play music, he simply goes over the day in his head. He debriefs the day, what went well and what he could have done better. As he gets halfway to his car, he switches off from work and starts to think about how he wants to show up when he gets in the door. What kind of a husband and father he wants to be. He said that the Third Space completely changed how he enters the home environment. He no longer feels like his family gets the worst part of him. When it's raining and he doesn't do the walk he can really notice the difference. He doesn't show up as well. The other bonus is that the 12-kilometre walk each day has given his health a huge boost, too.

GETTING TO KNOW YOUR PARTNER AGAIN

Some close friends of mine both work in the centre of Sydney. They used to live in an inner-city suburb. However, they recently moved south of Sydney to live on the coast. They now commute one hour a day on the train. They told me it's the best thing they have ever done for their relationship. They get to travel home together, and for this one hour they talk instead of working on their laptops or reading. They both said that they are learning new things about each other. Brilliant!

LEAVE IT IN THE POOL

Many years ago I was asked by Alan Thompson, the then head coach of the Australian swim team, to present to a group of elite swimmers in Year 12 who were considering stopping swimming to focus on their studies. I encouraged them to keep swimming as not only was it is important for them to have a focus outside of school, but the exercise would improve their brain function as well. Following the presentation one of the swimmers came up to me and told me how important the swim after school was for her. She said, 'When I miss the swim after school, school and study just blend into one big mess and I don't seem to be able to focus on studying so I get nothing done.' For her, the afternoon session was the Third Space where she could rest her brain and disconnect from the school day so she had a clear mind to focus on studying.

As you can see, the work-to-home Third Space can be anything. For some people, it's the car ride home. It may be the only time of the day where they are not responsible for another human being. It's their time to think about their world and play some relaxing music and change their mindset to one that will suit home. Alternatively, it could be as little as reading a book or listening to music on public transport.

CRUCIAL COMPONENTS

I believe that an optimal work-to-home Third Space is anything that involves any of the following four things:

1. *Physical activity:* when we exert ourselves physically we reduce the level of two hormones in our brain called adrenalin and cortisol. These shift us into a 'fight or flight' response, making it more difficult to regulate our behaviour and more difficult to empathise with others. If you go home with a head full of these two chemicals, you can guarantee fireworks at the end of the day. These two hormones are the reason you can be driving home thinking, 'I can't wait to see my family,' yet the first thing one of them says when you walk through the door makes you want to head-butt them. Moreover, physical activity elevates our mood, clears our thinking and allows our brain to focus.

2. *People we like:* humans are inherently social animals and we love to bond and interact. If we can bond with people and laugh between work and home it dramatically improves our quality of life.

3. *Relaxation:* by doing something that significantly relaxes us – yoga, walking home, meditation, reading, music or other methods of relaxation – our emotions, thoughts and behaviour become

calmer and composed, allowing us to bond with the people in our lives or simply unwind at the end of the day.

4. *A task that we get lost in and totally engaged with:* activities such as reading on the train, doing Sudoku or the crossword, playing a musical instrument, attending to pets, playing sport and so on. When the brain becomes focused it also becomes calm and less stressed.

For the remainder of the book we will cover exactly what we need to do on a mental level to get the most out of each Third Space. I encourage you to incorporate the preceding techniques in you transition between work and home.

PUT YOURSELF IN THEIR SHOES

If your home contains other people, in the transition from work to home, consider what has been happening for the people in that next environment. This is where the concept of empathy comes into play. Empathy is the ability to put yourself in someone else's shoes. The last thing I do as I approach my home is run scenarios of what might be going on for my wife. She may have had a day with a demanding, screaming child and may not have had a chance to get anything done. That will be very frustrating for her. She may also be just bone tired and need help and support to organise the house and feed Bella. Alternatively, she may have had the most amazing day and can't wait to share it with me. Running these scenarios helps you get in their head space and have an understanding of what might be greeting you in the Second Space.

While presenting to a group in Perth, a woman came up to me and said, 'I need your help! My husband works in the mines. He does two weeks on and two weeks at home. However, we fight for the first four days of him being home.'

I asked her what happened when he came home.

'Well I pretty much greet him with a to-do list of what needs to be done around the house. He then says he's been working his arse off and now that he's come home I expect him to do more work. That's when we start to fight.'

I asked her if she allowed him to have down time.

'Well, why should he get down time? I have to work full-time and for two weeks I have to do everything at home. Why should he get a break?'

When I asked her what she thought it was like for him to be away, she replied that it was horrible for him: having to work 16 hour days, share a room with the other guys and perform very physically tiring tasks.

'So how do you think he feels when he comes home?' I asked.

'He's probably exhausted and frustrated after having to live in those conditions,' was her reply.

I asked her to do me a favour and for the next three cycles let him come home and for two days watch TV and play video games on the lounge. She was not happy in the slightest and reminded me that she needed help and it wasn't fair.

'Do you want to be happy or right?' I asked.

'Happy,' she said.

'Then do it!'

When we spoke six weeks later she said it was remarkable. They stopped fighting and after the two days her husband came to her and asked, 'Hey, honey. What do you need me to do around the place?' Letting him transition back in his own way was crucial for their happiness.

CAN I PROVE IT WORKS?

Following a keynote I presented at the 2010 Australian Human Resource Institute (AHRI) Conference, John Molineux, a researcher from Deakin University, approached me. 'I love your Third Space concept,' said John. 'Well if you love it so much, let's do some research to prove how effective it is,' was my reply.

We designed a survey that explored how people currently transitioned home and had them rate what sort of a state they entered the home in. After they filled out the survey, they attended a one-hour presentation with me covering the Third Space, specifically explaining what the concept was, mapping out the Reflect, Rest and Reset phases (you're about to learn these in the next chapter) and providing case studies of people who transitioned from work to home effectively. Two weeks after the presentation, they were asked to complete a follow-up survey to measure any changes that occurred.

The first group we studied consisted of 102 small business owners. This is an interesting group because their work and personal life is constantly in a state of flux, with long work hours, competing demands and high pressure. If we could make a difference to these people, we could do anything.

The results of the first survey did not paint a pretty picture. There was a huge gap between how the group behaved in the home and how they wanted to behave. However, we were ecstatic to see that the incorporation of the Third Space had a very real and significant impact on the group. In the pre-survey, a whopping 89 per cent of them said that they wanted to come home in a positive state of mind; but only 26 per cent of those surveyed said they actually came home feeling positive. Following the seminar, this figure rose to 43 per cent. Woo hoo! Some comments people made in the follow-up survey included, 'Starting to think about being present', 'I try to switch off from work a lot more now and concentrate on home', 'Used to be pissed off when I came home' and 'Thinking less about work and more about my family.' 'Being single I now focus more on being relaxed when I come home, not working as much and spending more time socialising.'

Just as important, in the pre-survey only 39 per cent of people thought that their family/partner saw them coming home in a positive state of mind. In the second survey, 52 per cent of the participants believed their family/partner saw them as coming home in a positive state of mind. Comments included, 'When I am with my family I am much more present with them', 'I still do work at home ... but I now put aside pure family time when I turn off the phone and just spend time with them', 'I think my home environment has improved significantly, it is far less stressful' and 'I think they look forward to seeing me more.' 'My friends have commented that when I socialise with them I am much more relaxed, less distracted and nicer to be around.'

Finally, in the first survey 43 per cent of people thought they came home in a positive mood. This means exhibiting positive emotions such as calmness or happiness. This increased to 59 per cent of people walking in the door in a positive mood. Comments included, 'I am much happier when I come home', 'Used to be a grumpy old man' and 'I am much calmer as I used to be quite tense.'

While our research continues, this pilot study clearly shows that applying the principles of the Third Space has a positive impact on people's behaviour in the home environment.[1]

SUMMARY

What we do in the transitional space between work and home will determine how we show up when we enter the home environment.

The following are elements of an ideal Third Space between work and home:

- physical activity
- people we like
- relaxation
- a task that we get totally lost in.

Chapter 5

Check your baggage at the door – Reflect

Year Five was the very first time I looked at a girl and didn't think, 'Ew, girl germs.' In fact I started to think they were pretty cool. One day I even considered holding hands with one (of course, I didn't actually get to do it). The girl pressure was exacerbated by the fact that we were told we would need to have a partner for the end of school dance. Gee, talk about stress. In order to handle this pressure, In order to handle this pressure, we did what men always do when it comes to meeting women: we got a big group of us with no experience whatsoever together, then made up ridiculous strategies for how to do it. Ivan was howled down for his ludicrous idea of 'Why don't we just walk up ask whoever we want to take?' What an idiot! My mate Dave said, I'm going to bump into Cindy, then when I say "sorry", I'll ask her.' We all nodded at his brilliance, and then went off to turn the playground into a human dodgem car rink with little 9-year-old boys bumping into a very bemused bunch of girls.

With no success, eventually one of the guys in the group said he would go home and ask his older brother for advice. The next day we were all very

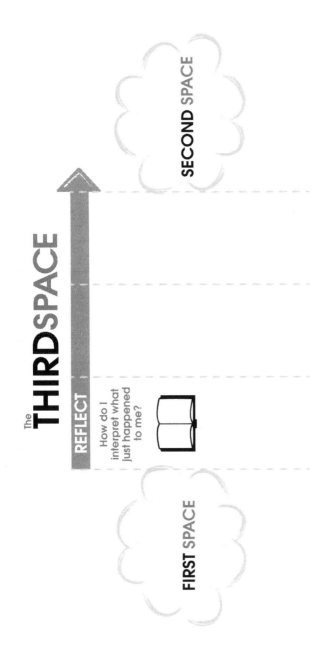

excited about the words of wisdom that would make this terrible task more bearable. When Nathan returned to school we asked, 'What should we do?'

'Mark reckons we should stay away from them.'

'Why?'

'Because girls have baggage!'

'What's baggage?'

'I don't know but it doesn't sound good.'

That was my first exposure to baggage. We all know that in society, baggage is a term that refers to the negative emotions and experiences from the past that we carry around with us, making our lives worse. 'I had to dump him because he's got too much baggage,' or 'I really like her but I just can't handle her baggage,' are all phrases we heard our friends say as we were growing up.

I see it in daily life, too. We have a fight with our partner or our manager is rude to us and we hang onto it. I see people give a disastrous presentation at work and then they cannot think of anything else for the rest of the week. Negative baggage can make us miserable and destroy our performance.

When I was at university, I would run exercise classes for the residents in the local retirement villages. One thing that struck me was how many of them still talked about fights they had had with people 40 years ago and how mad they still were about it. These women were holding onto so many things from their past that were still eating away at them. One of the most respected keynote speakers in the world is a woman called Amanda Gore. She has a great line: 'Holding onto resentment is like drinking poison and waiting for the other person to die.' So true.

The first phase in the Third Space is Reflect. This is where we learn from what we have just done and are able to leave that previous space behind so we can transition cleanly. In other words, the Reflect phase involves checking your negative baggage at the door.

The purpose of this phase is to:
- learn from the previous space
- carry positive experiences in the previous space over to the next space
- leave behind negative experiences in the previous space.

WHY WE NEED THE REFLECT PHASE

The reason we need the Reflect phase is due to our highly developed brain. One of the things that separates us from most animals is that we have a neocortex that is capable of complex thought. It allows us to be creative, to drive innovation, learn, control our behaviour and predict the future. While this is a great thing because it helps us to evolve and develop, this gift is a double-edged sword. Our ability to produce complex thought can lead us to reflect in an unhealthy way and create unwanted baggage.

In his book *Why Zebras Don't Get Ulcers,* Stanford University biologist Robert M. Sapolsky talks about zebras only having one stress in their lives – lions. If a zebra is at a watering hole and a lion comes out of the bushes trying to eat it, two things can happen – it escapes or it is eaten. If it gets eaten, stress is the least of its worries. If it escapes, by the time it stops running it has used up all the stress hormones that it released. In effect, when the zebra stops running, it's as if the stress never occurred. The problem with humans is that we get stressed behind the wheel of a car or at our desk and the stress hormones we release are never used up. They continue to float around our body, slowly killing us. The zebra's response to stress is perfect, hence the reason zebras don't get ulcers.

The other advantage zebras have over us is that after running away from the lion their small neocortex does not allow them to carry that baggage with them. What do they do when they stop running? They start eating the grass again. They don't huddle in a group and say, 'Oh my gosh, they got Barry. Can you believe it? Barry is dead. They are eating him right now. I can't stop looking over there.' There is no zebra off to the side saying, 'Not one lion tried to eat me. They never try to eat me. Is there something wrong with me? Do I run funny? I know I've let myself go after the last foal, but hey I'm a busy mum. Even the hyenas have stopped checking me out. I'm not even appealing to scavengers for God's sake.'

While zebras don't do this, we do – when we are rejected in a sales situation, a presentation we deliver receives poor feedback or our partner is quiet and withdrawn at dinner. Often our reflection can be unhealthy. Following these interactions we drive ourselves nuts overanalysing and worrying about what will happen next. I once heard a quote which said, 'My life has been full of tragedy, turmoil and disaster, some of which has actually happened.' The first step in transitioning is the ability to reflect accurately on the First Space and learn from it.

THE MASTER OF REFLECTION

Evelaine Berry, mid-career, decided to work as a community nurse. What struck her was the need for more support for patients (and their families) during their cancer treatment. She thought there must be a better way. There needed to be someone to explain to patients what their options were, to remind them that they had rights and to give them a sense of control. She had a dream to improve the support that patients received during their cancer journey.

Evelaine became the first Oncology Nurse Consultant for the Area Health Service. She helped people who were diagnosed with cancer and supported them through making decisions about their treatment and then into palliative care if it progressed to that. She helped link them with support groups and encouraged them to get involved in events where they could be with other people who were going through similar experiences. Evelaine didn't provide the treatments; her whole focus was how to support people at every stage of the cancer journey. She would even set up relaxation classes or art classes to help their mind, body and spirit.

Evelaine volunteered with Camp Quality, doing the same work with families and children. Because of her role, she would often support the families and the person with cancer at the time of their passing. She has been with countless families when and if a loved one died.

This is where I met Evelaine – working with Camp Quality. The best way to describe Evelaine is a 152-centimetre-tall ball of love. She is the grandmother everyone wishes they had, incredibly calm and composed yet with an unforgettable presence at the same time. The thing that stands out the most about Evy is her unwavering love for the children and the limitless joy she brings to people. The reason I particularly wanted to mention Evy in this book is that I cannot think of a harder role or environment to transition out of than hers. How do you transition from supporting a family that has lost what is most precious to them, to then going to work and doing admin, or going home and being with your own family? How does Evy check her baggage at the door so she can get on with her life and look after the next space? When I interviewed her I asked how she transitioned out of such a challenging situation. This is what she had to say.

'Firstly,' she said, 'you must acknowledge all your own reactions. Take time to reflect on what has just happened to you and how it has impacted you. It may be the loss you have experienced, the fact that a relationship with that person no longer exists, or the fact that you are angry at how unfair it is that the person was taken away. Don't brush it aside. Face it and recognise how it makes you feel. Realise, also, the times when you need to debrief.'

Evelaine often debriefed with co-workers or friends in the Third Space as a way to help her overcome and transition out of an emotional experience.

Debriefing is important for all of us. In my work I have come across teachers who work at a school that deals with children who have severe behavioural issues. At the end of each day, they get together as a group and debrief the day so they don't go home still reeling from having been kicked and punched and abused by the students. The communal debrief allows them to close that space.

Secondly, Evelaine stressed the importance of letting go of your reactions. She said every interaction we have with others involves having reactions to those people, to events, and to situations. For example, she may be dealing with the parent of a sick child and an internal reaction may come up where she thinks that there may have been a different way to do things, or a more useful decision could have been made. What is key is to let go of all those reactions, let go of the judgements and let go of the resentment. She says that holding onto those emotions impedes your ability to show up and help others in the next space.

Thirdly, Evelaine said, it was important to learn and reflect on what just happened. To ask yourself, 'What was I really happy with in that interaction? What could I have done better in that situation? What can I now do for that person to make things better for them?' Evelaine looked at every situation with gratitude. As she walked away, she always said to herself, 'What an amazing privilege that was. I'm really fortunate to have been there and maybe I was the right person to be there. I hope I made a difference.'

Finally, Evelaine is practical about the story she tells herself. She recognises that no one promised us that we would have a life that was free of pain, struggle and illness. Rather than striking out and blaming the world or other people, she realised that death is simply a part of life. She is incredibly pragmatic and realistic about her response. 'Sometimes you just have to accept that life is not fair and terribly sad things happen. Becoming resentful and angry simply hurts you and the people around you.'

In her role, it is never easy to lose someone and grief is always hard. You don't simply get over it. However, these specific steps she takes as she reflects on what she has just been through allow her to deal with it and transition into her next role or environment much more effectively.

At the end of our interview I asked Evy if she'd ever burned out.

'Oh, yes,' she said, 'many times. There have been times where I just had to get on a plane and say, "Get me out of here."'

But it wasn't supporting families of people with cancer that burned her out. She said it was the bureaucracy of work – the paperwork. The fact that her superiors were asking her to fill in case studies and give detailed notes when she knew she needed to be with a dying child rather than put pen to paper. Her effective transitioning allowed her to have longevity in a job that most people would not last a week in.

If this process helped Evelaine transition out of one of the hardest jobs in the world, surely it can help all of us transition cleanly into our own next space.

REFLECTING ON THE GOOD

When I first enrolled in university I was a self-confessed 'brain nerd'. I was fascinated by the brain and obsessed with trying to find out how the brain could help us perform better. Needless to say I was very excited about my very first lecture in psychology. To say I walked out of this lecture disappointed was an understatement – I was psychologically scarred. What I learned from this lecture was that we are all 'repressed' or 'screwed up' and that apparently I had an Oedipus complex thanks to my new friend Sigmund Freud. It didn't stop there. Week after week I became more aware of the fact that we are all nuts and that my dad should hide the kitchen knives. I wondered when we would get to the good stuff, when we would find out about making things better. All hope was lost when they introduced statistics.

Early on, I thought I wanted to be a clinical psychologist. In preparation for this, during first year I volunteered for every experiment and got to be involved in a number of research projects. During a conversation with one psychologist, I asked, 'What happens if someone comes to see you and they seem pretty happy and nothing is really going terribly wrong?' His response, I kid you not, was, 'Well at that stage, you ask a series of probing questions to uncover the real misery that underlines that facade.' Psychology constantly left me with a heavy heart.

Needless to say when the concept of positive psychology was born I immediately found resonance with it. While for centuries we have been talking about the concepts related to positive psychology, this concept was really given a framework and scientific backing by Martin Seligman, in particular, after writing a paper on the idea with Mihalyi Csikszentmihalyi.[1] Since then, many researchers have explored the role of positive psychology and how it can improve our happiness and quality of life.

It can be explained as follows: traditional psychology focuses on mental ailments and distress. In other words, how do we fix things so that people can return to 'normal'? How do we make people functional again? While it is incredibly important, especially for those with significant issues, traditional psychology really does have a focus on misery and dysfunction. Its purpose is to return people back to 'normal'. In contrast, positive psychology looks at how we use the same scientific prowess to help people thrive and have optimal functioning. How do people excel and flourish beyond their current position? How do we focus on people's strengths and virtues and then build on them for better happiness and well-being?

Positive psychology is about focusing on what is already going well and simply making it better rather than focusing solely on trying to fix what is wrong.

The first phase of the Third Space uses this theory to help each space make our lives thrive rather than just cope with or get over what we have just been through.

One thing I learned from the soldiers I have worked with is that they debrief and analyse the exercises they run. Not only do they look at what they need to do differently, they also look at what was successful and, most importantly, why. This same mentality is echoed in the principals of positive psychology. It's about consistently looking at what you are doing well and understanding why it went well so that you can repeat that be-haviour.

WHAT WENT WELL?

I once attended a workshop given by Dr Martin Seligman in which he talked about a technique called 'what went well'. It simply means that you spend part of the day reflecting on what went well. Cynics hear this and think it's far too fluffy. However, if you look at any research on this it will tell you that reflecting on success gives you optimistic thoughts and puts you in a state of positive emotion.

Conclusively, we know that positive emotion and optimistic thoughts accelerate learning, broaden attention and increase creativity. Also, over our lifetime if we consistently feel positive emotion and optimistic thoughts, we have better health, earn more money, have better relationships, and have a better quality of life.

Every time you enter the Third Space, the first question you need to ask yourself is what went well in the First Space? What did you just achieve?

You may be leaving a meeting, a presentation or an interaction with your partner or children. This gets you into a habit of acknowledging what you just achieved. It may be as trivial as 'I didn't procrastinate,' or as meaningful as 'I kept control of my temper when a colleague was being rude and critical of me.'

'WHAT WENT WELL' IMPROVES WORKPLACE CULTURE

This technique can also be applied at work to improve culture and achieve greater success. I was asked to present to a company called East Coast Bullbars, located north of Brisbane. As their name suggests, they make bullbars. They are an incredibly successful company that creates high-

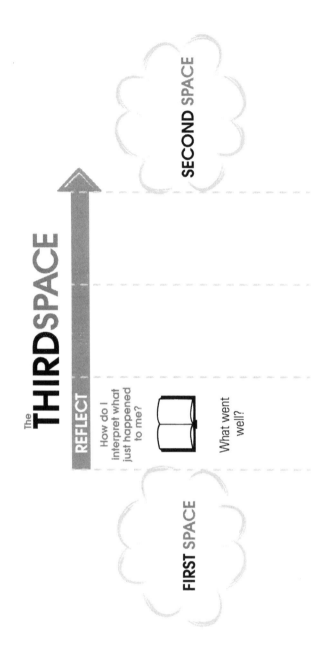

quality products. It's interesting, as a presenter, to notice the judgemental thoughts you may have about a group when you see them for the first time. When I walked in the room at East Coast BullBars, I noticed that the majority of the group were very tough-looking big guys who did not look like they were open to a conversation about their behaviour and emotions. I thought to myself, 'You could totally bomb in this room. These guys are not going to be into it.' My resilience then kicked in and I thought, 'Well if I'm going down, I'm going down swinging.' So I talked about the concept of 'what went well'. It was amazing. The whole group responded really well to the concept and one of them said, 'You know what, that is genius!' I was actually surprised.

'How is it genius?'

'I'm just picturing our weekly sales meeting. All we do is bitch about what went wrong the previous week, what we have to fix and what challenges are coming our way. Because of this, we walk out of the room very flat and defeated. We never reflect on what we do right and we do plenty right,' he said.

Then I asked the group to practically map out how they would implement 'what went well' into their organisation.

Six months later I emailed Ray, the managing director, to see how the team was going. This was his reply.

East Coast Bullbars – now almost six months on, some new vocabulary is really a part of the culture, some strong habits ingrained. Reference to good and bad performance is 'flow' and 'grind' etc. – The staff there are certainly more engaged, more days, more often – and it's influencing their performance.

'What did we smoke this week'[the renamed 'what went well' segment] *now a good habit and proving a*

good mechanism to focus on the positive at the end of a week – as the business already had an ingrained culture to review the problems.

What I love about this email (apart from the fact that they renamed 'what went well' to 'what did we smoke', clearly more manly, but unfortunately a statement that could be taken more than one way) is that they ingrained it into their culture and made it work. In follow-up conversations with Ray, he said the technique had a powerful impact on the team and that it had improved the culture significantly. Of all the companies I have worked with, ECB is one of the most impressive. They have a vision to be the world's best manufacturer of bullbars. They are terribly passionate about this vision and are using 'what went well' to build a culture that will get them there.

I introduced this habit in my own company and saw a dramatic lift in enthusiasm and positivity. You might consider starting off your meetings with a 'WWW'. Ask people to reflect on what they did well and report it back to the group. If you do this, I guarantee you that it will change the energy and optimism of the group. This is not 'fluffy stuff' – this leads to real business outcomes. Do this regularly and your team will be more focused on solutions, have greater self-belief and be much more highly engaged.

The key step with this technique is to ask the question: Why? Why did it go well? Ask what behaviour, process or practice made those things go well. This turns the technique from being superficial to practical. It gets them and you to cognitively recognise what actions lead to success. If you are consistently exploring what is driving constructive behaviour, there is a greater chance of you repeating that constructive behaviour.

What if you had a strategy where every time you met with a member of your team one-on-one, you began by asking them what went well? You then have them analyse why it went well and how they could use those skills in other areas. Finally, you gave them a specific area to focus on and develop those skills further. If you did that, do you think your team would like meeting with you? I think yes.

RECOVERING FROM INJURY

Gary Webb has a long history of working with people who have sustained a workplace injury. As an exercise physiologist his job is to physically rehabilitate them and assist in their return to work. Having had exposure to this role I know it can be soul-destroying. Many of the people you work with are very unhappy and many of them experience chronic pain. In addition, there are patients who don't want to get better as they are getting paid to stay at home. Gary and I caught up at a conference and discussed the benefits of positive psychology. He talked about a technique he used with most of his clients, particularly those who were certified totally unfit to return to work. It was called 'best and achieved'. Each day, as part of their rehab program, the client was asked to record the *best* thing that happened to them that day and what they had *achieved.* These were then discussed at the next appointment or follow-up phone call. What Gary pointed out was that he knew how quickly someone would return to work depending on how well they embraced 'best and achieved'. Regardless of their initial physical capabilities, people who took it seriously received work certificate upgrades and returned to work much quicker. Those who saw 'best and achieved' as unnecessary or stupid, and instead chose to focus on the negatives, normally failed to progress.

BEING CYNICAL DOESN'T HELP

I once gave a keynote presentation for a company that had a very functional culture and highly engaged leaders. Following the success of that keynote, they asked me to establish an ongoing program for them. In our first session we covered the 'what went well' technique. Each person created an action plan of how they would incorporate this technique into their personal and professional lives. They were pumped. Two months later we met again and reflected on this technique. The group were very excited about 'what went well'. There were countless stories of how it had improved culture, been fun, and how they had put their own personal spin on it. However, I did notice one group in particular giving each other cynical looks and raised eyebrows when the stories were relayed back. I asked them how they went with the technique. They very bluntly said, 'It didn't work and we thought it was silly.' What struck me was how different their behaviour and manner was to the other employees. They just didn't seem to fit. I relayed the story back to the business manager.

'Yes, they're our difficult group,' she said. 'They were hired by someone internally and didn't go through our cultural interview process to see if they fit our culture. In fact, they are our worst performing team because they are constantly criticising and gossiping about other people in the organisation.'

This is a pattern that I have seen repeatedly. The best teams embrace and love doing the 'what went well'. They see the value in it and see how it drives future performance. The dysfunctional, cynical teams do not. Yet every team that embraces this technique always sees an improvement in culture and, most importantly, profitability.

One challenge as a leader is that we often think we need to point out all the potential problems to team members, such as what they are doing wrong, in order to protect them or guide them along. However, this gets in the way of us supporting or celebrating with them. This does not mean you should be a pollyanna, never pointing out the potential issues. The best leader I ever had consistently focused on our strengths as a team and always got us to analyse how we were improving and look for other opportunities to apply those skills. She would also ask us about how we thought we could improve. In no way was she delusional – she would talk about mistakes we had made – but the balance leaned more towards what we were achieving and how we were getting better. Unfortunately, most leaders' feedback to their team is negative – focusing on what is not working and what the team needs to change to improve. This is a sure-fire way to guarantee a disengaged team.

DRIVE 'WHAT WENT WELL' INTO YOUR CO-WORKERS

You don't have to be a leader to use this tool. Get together with your colleagues and do it. At Glenallen School in Victoria, four team members, upon hearing about this technique, made a regular commitment to meet every Thursday at lunchtime where they discussed what they were achieving. Their regular get together has rules:

- It is a place of no judgement.
- They are able to give feedback without fear of persecution.
- They cannot complain about a situation without focusing on the solution.
- They focus on what they are doing well.

I asked the team to reflect on what they gained from these sessions. Their response was that these sessions are invaluable and have made an immeasurable difference to their lives. They said that not only had this led to a fantastic network of support at work, it also made them more resilient. Their ability to cope with challenges and setbacks has dramatically improved.

DO YOU CELEBRATE OR CRITICISE?

When you look at your relationships, how much time do you spend pointing out to your partner/friends/family what they're doing wrong? How much time do you spend talking about what they're doing right?

John Gottman is a researcher and co-founder of The Gottman Relationship Institute. He has spent his life studying what makes marriages succeed or fail. One of the glaring differences between relationships that thrived and relationships that fell apart was the ratio of positive to negative interactions. He found that relationships which excelled had a positive to negative ratio of 5:1. In other words they had five times the amount of positive interactions. However, failed relationships were found to have a ratio of 1:1.

POSITIVITY EQUALS PROFIT

Dr Marcial F. Losada from the University of Michigan has shown that for a corporate team to shift into high performance, it needs to hit a positive to negative ratio of 3:1. Teams below this were shown to flounder and be commercially unsuccessful. This means that to start to see success we need to have three times more positive interactions – comments, feedback and emotions – than negative ones. Three to one is the tipping point. However, his research also showed that if you were to take your team up to a ratio of 6:1, they'll shift into a new league of elite performance.

One of the reasons for this, apart from the fact that we need positive emotions ('what went well' leads to a state of positive emotion) to tap into our creativity and innovation, is that teams with low positivity ratios are very internally focused. They spend most of their time looking at the internal problems of the team and defending their actions and ideas, while being heavily critical of other people's actions and ideas. Teams with a low positivity ratio do not focus externally on innovation. In addition, teams with low positivity ratios don't question and challenge the way things are done – they simply try to protect their bit of turf. In contrast, highly positive teams are constantly challenging the status quo and devising new ways to do things. They are constantly looking externally to see how they can innovate and keep up with the new trends.

I see far too many managers use fear and guilt to manage their team. This only decreases their overall performance. Without positivity you will be left behind.

I often present with a speaker called Mike Walsh. Mike is the CEO of a company called Tomorrow and his speciality is understanding future trends. Specifically, he helps corporations prepare for the future and stay ahead of the competition. When we present together he informs the company of the new trends that will affect them, their industry or their profession. I then present on how they can embed new behaviours in the organisation to embrace these trends. We once presented at a conference for a company that used to be a Goliath in the business world. However, they are dying a slow death because the platforms on which people are accessing information have changed and they have not altered their business model. Neither Mike nor I could understand why they were not adapting.

Upon our arrival, Mike gave a compelling 45-minute presentation on the new trends in their industry. I followed with 45 minutes on the psychology of change and how they needed to lead their teams to help them embrace the new behaviours required to embed. Then we both sat on stage for 15 minutes of questions. How many questions did Mike get? Zero. How many did I get? Nine. All the questions I got were internally focused, petty issues: 'I have this guy in my team, no matter what I do I can't get him to engage and toe the line. What should I do with him?' 'My team just seems to fight all the time. We just have so much conflict. How can I stop this?'

There was our answer. Why weren't they innovating? They were an organisation that had a very low positivity ratio. Because of this, they were internally focused and never lifted their heads up and looked externally.

A friend of mine manages a sales team of 16 women. She is one of my favourite people, no fuss and a first-class manager. I asked her whether managing a team of a single gender is different to managing a mixed-gender team. She said, 'Society tells us that with many women in a team, there will be some personality clashes and some infighting. However, when I put this team together I simply told each person the core value of this team: 'We don't do drama.' If someone in this team has an issue they are to communicate it and come up with a solution. We do not tolerate people going behind other people's backs or being petty about issues. If someone is unhappy I will sit down with them anytime they want and discuss it, but we don't do drama. We are too busy and high-performing to tolerate drama.'

Having worked with corporate teams for over ten years, I've noticed that the difference between a poor-performing team and a high-performing team is that poor-performing teams are internally focused on bitch sessions and turf battles. Some teams I work with find it foreign and unusual to do 'what went well', which just shows us why there is so much unhappiness and dysfunction in their workplace.

'WHAT WENT WELL' IN ACTION

TravelEdge is an Australian-based company with a very positive culture. Its engagement scores and level of cohesion are the envy of many companies. Following a session where I talked about 'what went well', the people at TravelEdge embraced the concept whole-heartedly. Most importantly, each team took the concept and made its own version of it.

An akubra hat sits on a filing cabinet in the centre of one team. Throughout the day they write a little thank-you note when a team member has performed well and then place it in what they call their 'brilliance hat'. The hat collects these notes and at the start of their weekly team meetings the team members take turns reading out the comments that have been written. I asked one of the team members what impact this has had on the team. Her physiology simply exploded. She sat up straight and gesticulated wildly. 'It's amazing. Afterwards, we're all pumped. It brings the team closer together and our performance has really improved.' The other people in the team commented on how it put them in a cohesive, collaborative mindset for the rest of the meeting. They said it was just a little thing they do but it makes a BIG difference to the culture of the team.

The first step in Reflect is to look at 'what went well' in the previous space. Too often when we transition out of an event, we berate ourselves over what we stuffed up or what we could have done better. However, we rarely explore what we did well, why it occurred or how we can repeat that behaviour in the future. This is not about being delusional and ignoring what went wrong and what can we do better. Our interviews showed that people are already hardwired to focus on what they can improve. This is just adding another step that has been proven to improve performance and well-being.

As you enter Reflect, ask yourself 'what went well' in the previous space. This will balance out the natural tendency to ask what you did wrong in that space and how you can do things better.

HOW TO MAKE OUR RELATIONSHIPS ROCK

Some social research has suggested that our relationships are suffering. You only have to look at the extremely high divorce rates to realise that this includes our romantic relationships. In addition, we seem to have less time for friends and family. The premise of 'what went well' can have a profound impact on our relationships.

Dr Shelly Gable's research at UCLA[2] may have uncovered the secret to a successful relationship. Her research shows that the key to great relationships is celebrating actively with that person when something goes right for them. Think about this for a moment. When you have a positive experience your natural urge is to share this experience with the people around you. You want a witness, you want them to be as excited as you are. You want to bathe in the glory. This moment is a crucial opportunity to cement your relationships. What is interesting is that this type of celebration is not only good for the relationship, it is also important for the individual. The sharing of the positive event has been shown to have a greater impact on the person than experiencing the event itself. In fact, a person's life satisfaction measure is highest on days that they shared a positive event. If you want to improve your relationships, *never* minimise the importance of the other person's positive event or focus on the possible downsides.

People often think that we only bond over tragedy, that we strengthen relationships only when we counsel someone in bad times. However, a bond is also built when we help people celebrate a victory. I see this firsthand in my workshops. I ask people to reflect in pairs on a time when they've had 'flow' (this is a state in which they have been in 'the zone', whereby they perform a task in which they are completely immersed and do so successfully). They take turns coaching each other to describe what happened, the emotion they experienced, why they think they achieved 'flow' and how they felt afterwards. When I do this exercise I can feel the energy in the room lift. A noticeable bond develops between the pair coaching each other.

In Shelly Gable's research, she looks at the two levels on which a person can respond to another individual:

1. The energy you bring: active or passive.
2. The impact you have: constructive or destructive.

As you can see from the table below, these translate into four types of interaction:

	Constructive	Destructive
Active	Active/constructive	Active/destructive

	Constructive	Destructive
Passive	Passive/constructive	Passive/destructive

Active/constructive is giving the other person enthusiastic support.

Active/destructive is destroying or picking the event apart.

Passive/constructive is being supportive on a low level.

Passive/destructive is being dismissive of the event.

For example, your partner comes home and announces that s/he gave an amazing presentation at work.

Passive/destructive response – 'Yeah, right. Well that's great but my day was terrible. I'm going to lie down for a bit. I have a terrible headache.'

This statement would show that you're not involved (passive) and it is a destructive statement. It suggests that you think the event is insignificant and you don't care, and that your partner's thoughts and emotions are not important to you.

Participants in Dr Gable's study found to be on the receiving end of passive/destructive responses said the following about their partner:

- I get the impression that he/she does not care much.
- My partner doesn't pay much attention to me.
- My partner often seems disinterested.

Active/destructive response – 'That's great. Was your presentation on how to leave a kitchen in a complete mess? Because when I got home your breakfast crap was everywhere. I don't know how many times I have to tell you to put the plates in the dishwasher. I shouldn't have to come home and clean up your mess.'

In this statement you are involved, meaning you are engaging in the conversation (active) but it is a destructive statement – it completely removes any joy from the experience.

Those in Dr Gable's study found to be on the receiving end of active/destructive responses said the following about their partner:

- My partner often finds a problem with it.
- My partner reminds me that most good things have their bad aspects as well.
- S/he always points out the potential downsides of the good event.

Passive/constructive response – 'That's great honey. You really deserve it, well done.'

Even though this is a constructive thing to say, it is passive – you're just praising, not getting involved in what they have done. This statement does nothing to deepen the relationship.

People in Dr Gable's study on the receiving end of passive/constructive responses said the following about their partner:

- My partner tries not to make a big deal out of it, but is happy for me.

- My partner is usually silently supportive of the good things that occur to me.
- My partner says little, but I know s/he is happy for me.

Dr Gable's research showed that the above three approaches were negatively associated with relationship quality.

What you want to aim for is the following:

Active/constructive response – this means getting involved in the experience, helping them relive it, analyse it and learn from it.

'Wow, that's amazing! Tell me about what happened. How did that make you feel? What about it in particular went so well? Was your manager in the room? What did she think? What did you do that caused it to go so well?'

In effect, you are helping them relive the experience, to think about it deeply and to take that positivity and apply it to other parts of their life. In addition, you're reinforcing how important that event is and the statement shows that you care. Specifically, people who perceived that their partner responded in an active and constructive manner found that their relationship was of a higher quality, particularly in terms of intimacy.

Those in Dr Gable's study on the receiving end of active/constructive responses said the following about their partner:

- My partner usually reacts to my good fortune enthusiastically.

- I sometimes get the sense that my partner is even more happy and excited than I am.
- My partner often asks a lot of questions and shows genuine concern about the good event.

The study also found that couples who regularly had these interactions had lower levels of daily conflict.

Ask yourself: do I help the people in my life celebrate victory?

This research does not just apply to romantic relationships. It's just as applicable to your friendships. Do this with your friends and I guarantee your relationship will grow stronger.

ACTIVE/CONSTRUCTIVE AT WORK

What about at work? If you're a leader or manager, when you interact with your team do you only point out what they need to do better, or do you reflect and focus on what they have done well? Do you help them analyse and relive their victories? If you want to build closer bonds with your team members, this is a crucial habit to develop. Every manager that I have shared this model with and who has used it has reported dramatic improvements in the rapport they share with their team.

When your team is doing their 'what went well', do you actively engage in that discussion or are you acting passive/constructive by saying a few nice things and moving on too quickly?

If a member of your team comes to you and says, 'I've been looking at this system and I think it is really inefficient, but I've found a way that can streamline the process and save us both time and money', how do you respond?

Active/destructive – 'What are you messing around with that stuff for? That's not your key focus. We're under the pump here and you're screwing around with projects that aren't in our strategic plan. What, you don't have enough work to do?'

Passive/destructive – 'I don't have time to look at this right now. I am flat out.'

Passive/constructive – 'Good thinking. Let's chat about it later.'

Active/constructive – 'Great job. That process has been holding us back for ages. That is brilliant – great initiative. What do we have to do? Would you be able to lead this?'

What about your children? When they come up and show you a drawing they made just for you, how do you respond?

Active/destructive – 'Did you draw on the table? I've told you a million times not to do that. You'll leave marks on it.'

Passive/destructive – 'Don't interrupt me when I'm making dinner.'

Passive/constructive – 'That's great, baby. Looks beautiful. Can we look at it later?'

Active/constructive – 'Wow that's amazing. Is that a picture of a dog? ... Right, no, so that's a picture of me. That is beautiful, let's put your name on it and put it on the fridge.'

WHEN THINGS GO WRONG

It's important to have active/constructive conversations when things don't go right, too. One of the advantages of having a personal and romantic relationship is the ability to turn to this person when we are stressed or run into any of life's difficult challenges. The presence of social support is vital for someone to cope with stress and setbacks.

You come home to find your partner had a terrible day, thanks to a conflict with a co-worker. You could be passive/constructive. i.e., 'You'll be alright. Tomorrow's another day. What's for dinner?' But at this moment, you need to be active and constructive. Allow your partner to talk through it. Help them analyse the situation and focus on moving forward.

When people are suffering or struggling, be active and constructive in your responses. Ask them questions, be optimistic and listen actively. The key here is to steer the conversation in a positive direction. Here's an example:

Someone you work with presents an update on a project to the management team. They get absolutely grilled and it's obvious they were unprepared. Most people would tell them, 'You'll be okay.' (Passive/constructive.) However, if you are active/constructive and sit with them, help them analyse what went wrong and what they did well, and focus on what they can do to fix it, not only will that person feel better but your relationship with them will be improved.

One of the most important characteristics for a leader is to be consistent. If you have a team that is constantly wondering which mask their leader will be wearing that day, whether they'll be cranky, passive aggressive or friendly, then it's safe to say that the culture of your team will be dysfunctional.

To be a great leader you must ensure that when your team needs you, you engage in an active/constructive conversation. This approach is particularly important when you are having difficult conversations. Too often managers wait until they are angry or fired up to have difficult conversations with their team members. The reason is that they use the anger to propel them into this interaction. This is a recipe for disaster as the angry emotion clouds the manager's cognition and can lead to them saying things they did not mean (or send emails they wish they could get back). Being angry is a sure-fire path to destructive interactions.

Being a leader who strives to be active and constructive in his or her interactions is a vital step in creating a thriving and functional culture.

When someone with whom you want to have a strong relationship has a victory, be present, be curious and be enthusiastic.

SUMMARY

- The first thing we do when we enter the Third Space is Reflect on the First Space.
- Specifically, we reflect on 'what went well'. This allows us to learn from the First Space, minimise negative experiences and maximise positive experiences.
- This practice helps us keep constructive behaviours front of mind and increases our chance of repeating them.

Chapter 6

Tell your story walking!

POSITIVE THINKING DOESN'T WORK

Positive thinking has been the cornerstone technique of the pop psychology/self-help world since its conception. The rationale behind this technique is that to have a happy and successful life you need to think positively. Recently, the self-help world has gone through a new trend, which has taken this idea to the absolute nth degree. It is called the law of attraction. The theory is that if you want something, all you have to do is focus on it strongly enough and it will come into your life. Now, I'm all for focusing on what you want and being optimistic; however, I'm concerned about the message this sends. I think it gives people misconceived optimism: 'All I have to do to get that dream job is sit at home on the lounge and just want it badly enough.' It also implies that anyone can have anything they want – all they need to do is manifest it. I do have to admit, just thinking about piles of money appearing has worked incredibly well for the people selling the idea of the law of attraction, but for the rest of us it doesn't seem to work quite as powerfully. What this theory forgets to mention is that most people struggle for years and years and have to work their butts off before they see any sign of success. People often walk out of motivational seminars wanting to quit their jobs and start a new business. In reality, the majority of them do not have the skills, knowledge or necessary planning to do so. We need to be realistic about our capabilities. I may desperately want to play power forward for the LA Lakers, but no amount of manifesting will get me there (if you've met all 168 cm of me, you'll understand why I will never make it). I have seen this delusional thinking do great damage to people's lives. 'Realistic' is not a dirty word.

While I was researching this book, I was interested in finding out whether there was any real research showing that positive thinking works and leads to a better life. I was surprised with the results.

In 2009, Joanne Wood and her team conducted an experiment at the University of Waterloo. Using the Rosenberg Self-Esteem Scale, Joanne divided a group of people into three bands of selfesteem. The top band had high self-esteem, the middle band moderate self-esteem and the last band had low self-esteem. Participants were then asked to repeat positive affirmations to themselves. In other words, they were asked to practise positive thinking, saying things like, 'I am a lovable person'.

The researchers then remeasured the group's self-esteem following the positive thinking exercise. The results showed that the group with high self-esteem felt slightly better about themselves after saying positive affirmations. What was fascinating, though, was that after the exercise, the group with low self-esteem saw a significant drop in their self-worth. The group that didn't need more self-worth had a slight improvement, while the group that needed it the most were devastated by this technique.

Why, you ask? The reason is that for the group with low self-esteem, these statements were too far outside their self-image. Their brain rejected the statement and refuted it with a contradicting negative message that was aligned with their self-image. We all have a self-image. It is our view of ourselves and how we fit into the world. Our self-image is vitally important to us – even if it is negative – and we will fight tooth and nail to keep it intact. For example, if the positive affirmation was, 'I'm a loveable person', the thought pattern of a person with low self-esteem would be, 'No, you're not. And here's the evidence to prove it.' 'I am a good, honest person' becomes, 'no you're not. You haven't had a relationship in seven months, you broke your diet again at lunch today, you backstabbed Jenny to Katie today, and...' After their brain recites a series of negative dialogue to confirm their current self-image, they feel worse about themselves. When a positive statement does not line up with our self-image, we not only dismiss this statement but also strengthen and reinforce what we already 'know' about ourselves. This evidence suggests that self-helps books that focus on positive affirmations are not only ineffective, they're actually causing damage.

So what's the alternative? You need to understand your explanation style and ensure that the stories you tell yourself are accurate, realistic and optimistic.

WE COMMUNICATE AND LEARN THROUGH STORIES

I was once working with a company that completely turned its culture around and somehow got its employees to become attached to purpose and meaning within their roles. I asked the CEO how he drove this change. He simply said, 'By telling stories. People remember and emotionally connect to stories. It's a vital technique for helping people change their behaviour.' He's right. We connect and communicate with others through story. I find that in my presentations, the use of story is a hugely powerful tool to help people learn and remember what I'm teaching them. It's engaging. People get restless when bombarded with too much theory. But when you're telling a story they focus and engage deeply. We also communicate with ourselves through story. During the day, that little voice inside our head is running dialogue constantly to try to explain and interpret the world and events to ourselves.

I very clearly remember the day I had to tell myself the story that would make or break my career.

Early in my presenting career I was asked to speak at a conference to around 800 delegates. Because it was such a big conference, the stage had been elevated about a metre in the air. On stage left there were four steps down to the ground, and there were no steps on stage right. Unfortunately, during the morning session the globe in the projector hanging from the ceiling had blown and there was no replacement globe. As a solution, they rolled out an old projector that sounded like a jet engine taking off. It was placed on a table in front of the stage and projected onto the screen. The challenge was that the stage was only slightly wider than the screen and because the projector was on the floor, I couldn't stand on most of the stage because the projector would blind me every time I looked at the audience. The result: I had only a 60-centimetre square on stage right to use. In my presentations I also use a flip chart, so the flip chart and I were confined to this small area on the side of the stage. I thought about raising it with the conference organiser, but took one look at her and her expression said it all. She clearly had a lot on her plate and did not need me to add to her load. As a professional presenter you endeavour to make the conference organiser's life easier. Rule number one of presenting: don't ever whinge. You can be the greatest presenter in the world on stage, but if you are a pain in the arse off stage, that is all they will remember.

I began the presentation and it was going great, even though I felt like a caged lion stuck there in my 60-centimetre square of space. The audience was into it, I was into it. And then I wrote something on the flip chart and stood back to look at it. My foot was now at the point where my brain thought the stage should be ... except there was nothing but thin air. That's right. I stepped too far and off the stage. I leaned back at the same time so my centre of gravity went beyond the point of return.

Now gravity is not just a good idea, it's the law!

I began to fall.

But then my survival instincts kicked in – the primitive part of my brain, the one responsible for the 'fight or flight response', said, 'Grab onto something to break your fall.' I saw my left hand shoot out and grab hold of the flip chart.

Unfortunately, however, the weight of the flip chart pulled my body into a pike position and the rotational force spun me as I fell. The centrifugal force caused me to throw the flip chart away from my body like a frisbee. It was like something out of a Jackie Chan film.

Afternoon tea was next to the stage. There was a long table with an urn, glasses, sandwiches, and jugs of water on it. I threw the flip chart in such a way that it bounced across the top of the table, destroying everything it hit.

I landed on the ground with such force my battery pack for the lapel microphone jammed itself into my floating ribs, cracking one of them. I couldn't breathe.

Now that wouldn't have been so bad. However, as I lay there like a broken pretzel, all the water from the smashed jugs cascaded off the table and all over me – just to add insult to my significant injury.

As I lay there, almost unconscious, what did the audience do? Laugh! It was the biggest laugh of my career. There I was: embarrassed, hurt, wet through to my bones, and in front of 800 people. How could I have responded to that? I could have gotten angry. I could have succumbed to the humiliation.

Instead I said, 'I will now take questions from the floor.'

I once told this story in a workshop. One man suggested, 'You could have pretended it didn't happen.' Yeah right.

Later, I went over the stage incident again in my head. There were a couple of ways in which I could have responded to it:

Adam, you are such a screw up. I can't believe what a loser you are, you always embarrass yourself. In fact, just when things start to go well for you, something always goes wrong. Why do you even bother? You're not cut out for presenting and you will never make it. In fact, your life sucks. Running a business is too hard. You're simply pushing against the ocean.'

Or:

'Wow, that was so embarrassing, I can't believe that happened. That will make a great story. Brilliant material. You can't make a story like that up. You were such a trooper getting back up and finish-

ing the presentation, cracked rib and all. I know they laughed but you really won their respect. You just had a bad day. If you look at the grand scheme of things, you have had a great year. I know that today was embarrassing but overall you are doing really well.'

The story I chose to explain that event to myself had a massive impact on what would happen next. The story we tell ourselves determines whether we will carry that event with us for years or stay resilient to it and move on. They are crucial to our happiness, well-being and resilience.

This brings us to the second part of Reflect, where you ask the question: what story will I tell myself about what just happened to me?

PLEASE EXPLAIN

The best work I have come across around explanation style was in the book *Learned optimism: How to change your mind and your life* by Dr Martin Seligman.[1] What he talks about in this book is the importance of a healthy explanation style around how we explain setbacks, victories and daily events to ourselves. Specifically, the book points out that when we experience events in our day, we explain them to ourselves on three levels:

1. How *permanent* it is: how often that event occurs, i.e. it occurs all the time so it is permanent, or it rarely occurs so it is temporary.

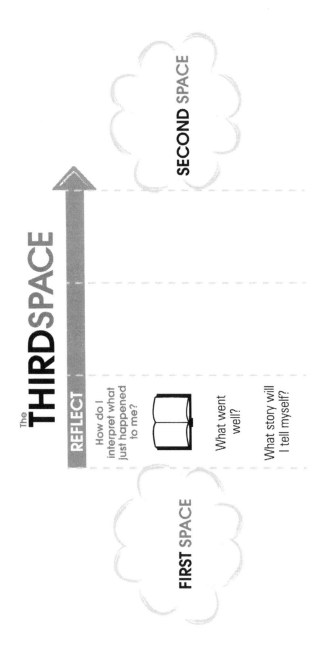

2. How *pervasive* it is: how much of our life that event affects, i.e. it affects everything so it is global, or it affects very little so it is specific.

3. How *personal* it is: whose actions caused the event to occur, i.e. it is due to me so it is internal, or it is due to others so it is external.

These are represented in the diagram below.

In other words, when an event occurs to us we can explain it by saying:

'Does this always happen to me or does this rarely happen?'

'Does this affect every area of my life or does it affect only a small part of my life?'

Level of Permanence
How Permanent is the event?

"Always Happens"
It is Permanent

"Rarely Happens"
It is Temporary

Level of Pervasiveness
How much of my life does it affect?

"Affects Everything"
It is Global

"Affects Little"
It is Specific

Level of Personalisation
Who caused the event to happen?

"Due to Me"
It is Internal

"Due to Others"
It is External

'Is this due to my actions or the actions of others?'

Our explanation of these three levels can sit anywhere on each spectrum.

What Seligman's research shows is that explanation style has a significant impact on our resilience, physical and mental health, our ability and our relationships. In addition, our explanation style determines whether we are optimistic or pessimistic.

WHEN OPTIMISTIC PEOPLE HAVE A 'GOOD' EVENT

When optimists experience a 'good' event, they explain it in the following way:

Permanent: 'This always happens to me.' I always do great presentations; I always convert my sales opportunities; I always lead my team well.

Global: 'This affects every part of my life.' I am very athletic; I am great at my job; I manage relationships really well.

Internal: 'It was due to my actions.' I did a great job of leading my team; I really motivated them and got them together; I am an excellent parent.

WHEN OPTIMISTIC PEOPLE HAVE A 'BAD' EVENT

When optimists experience a 'bad' event, they explain it in the following way:

Temporary: 'This rarely happens to me.' That presentation didn't go very well but the next one will be great; I had a bad round of golf – that is rare for me; I lost my temper with my mother. I rarely do that.

Specific: 'This affects very little of my life.' I am not getting along with that person right now; I called at the wrong time; I had a bad day at work today.

External: 'It was not due to my actions.' The problem with my presentation was the audience and the badly set-up room; it's my team's fault that we underperformed on this project; my partner was in a bad mood. That's why we argued.

> ***Note:* Optimists have to take extra care to be realistic about their involvement in failure due to this tendency to externalise failure.**

Outstanding leaders, parents, friends and partners always look at their behaviour first to see how it contributed to the situation.

Let's now look at the other end of the spectrum – the pessimist.

WHEN PESSIMISTIC PEOPLE HAVE A 'GOOD' EVENT

When pessimists experience a 'good' event, they explain it in the following way:

Temporary: 'This rarely happens to me.' I got lucky; it won't go so well next time.

Specific: 'This affects very little of my life.' Yeah, I had a good day, but the company is struggling at the moment and the economy is slow so I'll probably lose my job.

External: 'It was not due to my actions.' That other person really helped me with that project; it was a team effort; the client was in a good mood, which is why the meeting went so well.

WHEN PESSIMISTIC PEOPLE HAVE A 'BAD' EVENT

Conversely, when pessimists experience a 'bad' event, they explain it in the following way:

Permanent: 'This always happens to me.' I always make mistakes; I'm constantly screwing up; I never get along with my co-workers.

Global: 'This affects everything in my life.' I am terrible at relationships; I'm just not very smart; nothing ever goes right for me.

Internal: 'It was my fault.' I'm a terrible public speaker; my team underperformed because of my bad leadership.

Keeping these types of explanation styles in mind, let's go back to my stage incident. If I were pessimistic, I could have told myself things always went bad for me (permanent) and that I was such a klutz and loser (global and internal). Instead I reacted optimistically. I told myself that this was the first time I'd ever fallen off a stage (temporary), that I was simply having a bad presentation day (specific) and that the stage set-up was always going to lead to disaster (external).

Your explanation style will determine how quickly you bounce back from an event and whether or not you end up carrying that baggage with you.

Seligman, in his book, encourages us to monitor and regulate our explanation style and ensure that it is accurate, realistic and optimistic.

YOUR EXPLANATION STYLE IS OFTEN INACCURATE

After being exposed to this model I started to see explanation style everywhere.

I was on a flight travelling business class. At the start of the flight, a crew member collected the suit jacket of the man next to me and hung it up. Generally, when you give your jacket to them, you put your boarding pass in the pocket so the crew can return it to you easily. On this flight, after the plane landed, the man next to me very rudely said to one of the crew, 'Where is my jacket?' 'Sorry, sir,' she said. 'It didn't have a boarding pass in the pocket so I didn't know who to give it to. I'll just grab it now for you.' He then turned to me and said, 'She could have at least told me that I needed to put it in the pocket. I hate this airline. The service is terrible and the staff are always rude (as well as a few choice words that I won't print here).'

The reality was that there was a simple breakdown in communication. Yet his explanation of the event was:

External – their fault completely
Permanent – the staff are always rude
Global – their service is terrible

Now this may seem like a trivial example, but if this was his explanation style for something so insignificant, imagine how he might explain it when one of his staff makes a mistake or his kids behave poorly.

EXPLAINING YOUR SALES PERFORMANCE

A friend of mine, Chris, works in sales and coaches sales teams. When I showed him this explanation style model, he was able to see that those struggling in the teams he coached had the following, pessimistic, style:

'I am hopeless at sales.' (Global and internal)
'I always get rejected.' (Permanent)
'People always say no.' (Permanent and global)

Those in the teams performing well in sales, on the other hand, said:

'I get some "no's", but that's sales for you. When you get a "no" you just move onto the next one.' (Temporary)

'Some people are just not in the right space to buy.' (Specific)

'No matter what you do some people will always say "no".' (External)

Chris started using this model to challenge his team's explanation styles. When they say, 'I always get rejected', he replies, 'How accurate is that? You never get a sale? Really?'

To which they reply, 'Oh, well, it's not like I never get a sale but I get a lot of "no's".'

'Well look at your results. You only just missed out on budget this month, which tells me you must have got a lot of "yes's", too. What are you doing differently when you get a "yes" compared to when you get a "no"?...'

When we caught up, Chris remarked on what a difference the use of explanation style made to his sales coaching process and what a useful tool it was for people to take away.

Metlife, an insurance company in the US, decided to work with its sales team using explanation style. When they examined their workforce, they found that the salespeople who were optimists sold close to 40 per cent more than the pessimists. On the back of these results they trialled a hiring process on a team of salespeople that was based on nothing other than explanation style. In the first year, this team outsold the others by 21 per cent and in the second year by 57 per cent.

NEW PARENTS

As anyone with children will testify, when you become a parent you find yourself completely out of your depth. It's a huge rollercoaster ride. All those day-to-day changes combined with sleep deprivation can easily lead to a poor explanation style. After we had our first child, I noticed both my wife's and my explanation style became pessimistic. We would say things like, 'I can never do anything right. I'm just not cut out for this. When is it supposed to get easy? It's just not fun. I didn't achieve anything today.' It had a huge impact on our behaviour and our mood. Our negative explanation style led to us feeling defeated and deflated, our energy levels dropped and our enjoyment also dropped. The reality was that we were doing an amazing job and achieving things every day, yet we weren't explaining it that way. When we became more aware of our language and began to explain our situation in a more realistic and hopeful way, we started to feel better.

The more I became aware of it the more I noticed that most people's explanation style is pessimistic, inaccurate and unrealistic. People tend to make these sweeping statements that have no real truth to them. In workplaces I've heard things like, 'Yeah, our IT department is hopeless. They never get anything right.' Or, 'He's a disaster. Everything he touches he screws up.' People were not being reasonable in their explanation style. I also noticed that their explanation styles skewed their perception and ultimately impacted on their behaviour.

I recognised it in myself, too. I had developed a bad explanation style when I talked about our daughter. Bella is a very strong-willed child who often challenges us. (Our friends tell us that this is karma, as Chris and I are quite energetic, determined people.) When people asked me how our daughter was going, I would respond with, 'Oh my gosh, she's so full-on; her behaviour is so difficult. It's such a struggle.' My explanation style had become global, permanent and external. Chris eventually pulled me up, saying, 'It's really distressing when you do that. She is strong-willed but that is a great thing and she is not always difficult. In fact she is rarely difficult.' The language I had used was skewing my view of her and giving me a negative mindset.

I started not only challenging my explanation style but also that of the people around me. I was over at a friend's house one evening. His wife was asking him to do something over and over again. He turned to me and said, 'My God she always nags me. She just nags me about everything, day and night. She's driving me crazy!'

This statement is:

External – 'She's driving me crazy.'

Permanent – 'She always nags me.'

Global – 'She just nags me about everything.'

Rather than agreeing with him I said, 'No she doesn't.' That got his attention. 'What did you say?' I replied, 'She doesn't always nag you. She only nags you when you don't do what you said you would do, or when you ignore her.' He gave me a look that was a combination of 'get stuffed' and disbelief and then left the room. When he came back, we discussed it and I told him about explanation style. After a delicate conversation he had to agree. I asked why he had said what he said. His response was, 'I don't know, never thought about it. I guess I just focused on that one example. Also, it feels good to complain about her from time to time and feel that I'm in the right. Actually, I think I'm annoyed at her for something else and it's coming out now.'

What I found was that when people took the time to challenge these sweeping statements, their perspective of the situation changed. They often calmed down and became much more reasonable. When we experience challenging events, we can sometimes fall into the trap of going to either extreme, such as making things permanent or global when they are not. The most resilient people and the best performers are able to regulate their explanation style.

EXPLANATION STYLE CAN MAKE YOU RESILIENT

I was presenting at a conference with another speaker who was very successful and quite well regarded. We were both speaking to a large bank. I'm not sure what happened but halfway through his presentation, he started referring to their major competitor. He had forgotten which bank he was talking to. You could see the CEO's reaction: he was not impressed. The speaker got off stage and realised what he had done. He looked at me and said, 'I can't believe I did that. What a huge screw-up.' I checked back in with him 30 minutes later and asked how he was feeling. He said, 'Fine! I think I'm a bit jet-lagged and hey, you do 150 of these things a year, you're bound to mess one up from time to time. It's not ideal but it's not the end of the world. I've never done that before and I will make sure it never happens again'.

He could have so easily blown that out of proportion and beaten himself up. However, his explanation style involved taking this bad event and making it temporary (I've never done that before and I will make sure it never happens again), specific (bound to mess one up from time to time) and external (I think I'm a bit jet-lagged).

ACCURACY, REALISM AND OPTIMISM

Every time you transition out of the First Space you have to be careful to monitor your explanation style to ensure that it is accurate, realistic and optimistic. The aim, as we saw from the examples above, is to strike a balance. Blind optimism, to the point of delusion, can get you in just as much trouble as melancholy pessimism.

WHEN YOU GO TOO FAR: BLIND OPTIMISM

I was once asked by a school to speak at their staff day about improving the team's performance. As I was preparing to present, the principal walked in and introduced herself. I said, 'Before I present, is there anything else I need to know about the group?'

'Yes,' she replied. 'I don't want you to talk about stress, pressure, burnout, conflict or challenges.'

Wow, I thought to myself. I have nothing left to discuss! I asked her why she didn't want me to mention any of those things. She slammed her hand down on the desk.

'Because no one in here is stressed. Everyone is happy here. We don't have excessive workloads, we are an employer of choice, our culture is great and I don't want you putting stupid ideas in their heads that something may be wrong.' As she left the room I turned to the assistant principal.

'Is it really like that here?'

'No, it's not at all,' she replied. 'The problem is she won't let us talk about any issues because she refuses to acknowledge that there are any.' The principal's delusional optimism was actually creating a dysfunctional culture.

I once worked on a project with a very successful young entre preneur who had the most unique explanation style I've ever come across. We were chatting one day when he turned to me and said, 'You know that negative voice inside your head that tells you that you can't do things, do you have one of those?' 'Yeah, of course I have one of those,' I replied. He said, 'I don't think I've got one.' He once called me from London and said, 'You'll never guess who I just followed at a conference.' It was Bono, lead singer of the band U2. This young entrepreneur had just met him. I said to him, 'Wow. Eleven years ago when you left high school, did you think you'd be doing this?' 'Yep,' he said. 'I was always going to make it!' This one individual made 946 sales calls before he received one yes to start his business. How do I know this? He logged each call in a spreadsheet. Just pause and think about that – 946 people told him they did not like his idea before he got one yes. Yet he still picked up the phone. Personally, if I got even three rejections I'd be in the corner in the foetal position, sucking my thumb. Why did he keep picking up the phone? It came down to his explanation style.

He explained the rejection in the following way.

Temporary – 'The next one will say yes.'

Specific – 'So what? That one person can't see the value in it. That doesn't mean it is a bad idea. It just doesn't appeal to them.'

External – 'Can't they see that this is the future? Can't they see that this will revolutionise the way we look at the workforce?' (He was right, by the way. His idea was amazing and before its time.)

While this explanation style made him incredibly successful and resilient, an extreme explanation style like this can also be dysfunctional. One of the ways in which it manifested itself was the way he treated people, particularly his staff. His organisation had a huge turnover rate, and very few people could handle him. Why? Because when they made a mistake, whose fault was it? Theirs, of course. When they made mistakes, he would externalise the responsibility for them to his staff. He had to dramatically work on his behaviour and treatment of others. He's still very resilient to setbacks and challenges, but is now much more accurate and realistic about how he explains the world.

GET IT WRONG, NEXT STOP BURNOUT

Extreme pessimism is damaging, too. I was asked to coach a manager in an organisation, but before we were able to meet up he had a nervous breakdown and was carried out of work by paramedics in a full-blown panic attack. I finally had a chance to work with him when he returned to work seven months later. This was a hugely successful individual. In every organisation he had worked with he set revenue records. But when we had our first meeting, I discovered that his explanation style was strongly biased towards pessimism. He made his success temporary with statements such as, 'Well you're only as good as your last project,' or, 'It's only a matter of time before you make a big mistake.' He made his success specific: 'The margins are getting tighter, the economy is so slow at the moment, competition is fierce and we have made some poor decisions. Sure, I've had a couple of wins in the past but they mean nothing. It's a new world and the playing field has changed.'

When I challenged him on this and talked about what a great performer he was, he externalised his success. 'I've been very lucky. I always have great teams behind me and supportive managers. Most of the deals I made were a matter of being in the right place at the right time. My luck is bound to run out soon.'

His explanation style never allowed him to relax and enjoy a victory. He was convinced that the next mistake was just around the corner, that things were going to get much worse and his luck would run out. No wonder he felt the stress so much.

When you transition out of each space, ensure that the story you tell yourself is accurate, realistic and optimistic.

SUMMARY

- Repeating positive affirmations to yourself has been shown to have little effect and, in many cases, a negative impact on your self-worth.
- We interpret the world through stories that we tell ourselves about events and situations.
- We explain events/situations on three levels:
    -how permanent it is (permanent or temporary)
    -how pervasive it is (global or specific)
    -how personal it is (internal or external).
- Many people have an inaccurate, unrealistic and pessimistic explanation style.
- To improve our ability to transition out of the First Space, we need to ensure that the story we tell ourselves about the First Space is accurate, realistic and optimistic.

Chapter 7

Take it when you can get it – Rest

The next phase of the Third Space is Rest. This is where we have a moment of stillness to focus, become present and prepare ourselves for the next space. This moment may last two seconds as you duck between meetings or a couple of hours as you read a book in the backyard. No matter how long it lasts, rest is essential.

GOING FLAT OUT

I was presenting for a corporation at a conference in Barcelona and, as part of the whole experience, they asked me to stay for the full four days of the conference to get to know the group and work with them on a deeper level. The beauty of this was that I came to know the group really well and understand their challenges before I presented to them. One of the women in the group was an incredibly high-energy person who was very intense in everything she did. She was all about getting things done quickly and achieving results. This observation was reaffirmed in her language, her gestures, and even the way she walked. In fact, I was in the gym with her one morning and she was exercising so hard I thought her head was going to explode. I noticed during the conference that people kept telling her to do less and slow down.

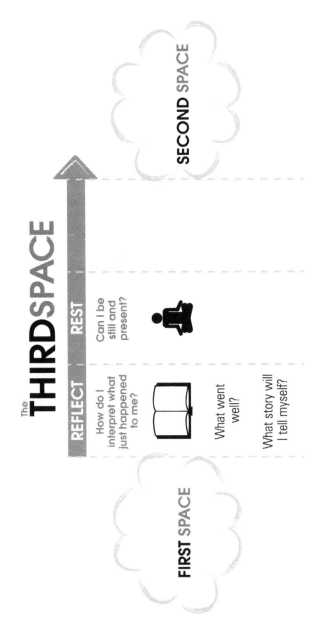

'You have to worry about burning out. You can't keep this pace up!' they kept saying. She was the brunt of many jokes about her fast-paced and crazy life. It was fascinating to observe her over the four days. At the conference dinner, I asked her if she ever burnt out.

'No,' she said, 'that's the thing. I've never burnt out yet people keep telling me that I will.' We discussed the possible reasons she could maintain her incredible pace. 'I think it's because at the end of every day, I come home, play some Ministry of Sound on my iPod, run a bath with some lavender bath oil, light some candles and just wind down. I completely turn off and relax. I don't answer 27 emails about missed orders and cancelled meetings, I don't look at what colleagues are having for dinner on Facebook; I don't even glance at my Blackberry. As soon as I walk through my front door it's like I shed my skin and become a totally different person. I am calm, relaxed and slow.' This is why she doesn't burn out: she builds recovery into every part of her day.

PREVENTING BURNOUT

When I was at the Australian Institute of Sport in Canberra, I had lunch with one of the scientists from the physiology lab. We were talking about a certain athlete and how well she was performing.

'Now we just need to ensure she doesn't get sick before the world championships,' the scientist said.

'Why would she get sick?' was my puzzled reply.

'Athletes are always on the verge of over-training or under-training. Unfortunately, if you over-train an athlete, their immune system starts to drop, they get sick and their overall performance suffers. Obviously we don't want that to happen. Here in Canberra we get it more right than most. We work them hard but we also rest them hard.' He then went on to describe that when his team was researching burnout in athletes they found that the key to preventing burnout was not flogging an athlete until they felt burnt out and then following that with long periods of recovery. Rather, the key to preventing burnout was short, regular, consistent bursts of recovery. The scientists would give the athletes an afternoon off occasionally, or would ensure that every athlete had a period of time each day to practise meditation or relaxation. He told me that many coaches push their athletes as hard as they can and then rest them only if they feel burnt out. 'What we do here is ensure they never get to that point by giving them short, regular and consistent bursts of recovery.'

I have applied this principle in the corporate world. When I work one-on-one with executives, the best model we have found to safeguard executives against burnout is this:

Each day they do something for at least ten minutes that completely relaxes them (reading, yoga, meditation, stretching, listening to relaxing music).

Each week they do something for at least one hour that re-energises them (e.g. getting a massage, walking on the beach, a relaxing breakfast, a hobby or spending time with friends).

Each month they have a lazy day where they have no responsibility, no time schedule and nothing organised.

Each quarter they have a long weekend where they completely relax and turn off.

This model, coupled with a holiday once a year, has had phenomenal success with preventing burnout and helping executives recover from burnout.

EXHAUSTION IS A BADGE OF HONOUR

The above model makes sense and works. So why do we struggle with doing it? Because we wear exhaustion as a badge of honour. We look at the idea of taking regular short bursts of recovery and think that is for weak people who can't handle the pressure, or that having these regular moments of stillness is self-indulgent and selfish. We found with most people that unless they were feeling exhausted and stressed, they didn't think they were pushing themselves hard enough. The culture of our workplaces also reinforces this type of attitude, because unless you are dragging yourself through the day, you're considered lazy. One of my favourite episodes of *Seinfeld* was when George Costanza figured out that all he had to do at work for people to think he was working hard was to look busy and annoyed. He literally did no work but every time someone walked past his office he would slam down the phone, kick the bin and throw things. After a week of this they promoted him.

This attitude is far too common in the workplace. When I spoke to people who were feeling burnt out, they would say things like, 'Yes I'm feeling burnt out but don't worry, I have a holiday in three months so I will cane myself till then and then I'll relax.' This is not sustainable high performance as these long periods of down time are far too infrequent.

In my experience, to prevent burnout and improve well-being we need short, regular and frequent moments of stillness. To shine some light on this we need to move out of the world of science and instead learn from ancient philosophy.

DIFFERENT ENERGY STATES

Eastern philosophy teaches us that there are three forms of energy we move between. First of all there's tiger energy, or high energy: fast and adrenaline-inspired, such as work, socialising or high-energy sports. Next, there's swan energy. This is where you are still and focused, calm but alert. It could involve meditation, a relaxing hobby, reading or conversation. Finally, we have sloth energy. This is where you are still and inert, for example, watching TV or sleeping.

It's easy to imagine a sloth-like person or tiger-like person, but we rarely see swan-like people as it takes a lot of effort and a heightened level of self-awareness. In the corporate world I see so much tiger energy; I think most people in this world try to exist on that form of energy alone. Eastern philosophy states that we cannot exist continually in one form of energy. Existing for too long in one type of energy is a recipe for disaster. While it's great to be fast-paced and vibrant (tiger), we need to intersperse that with activities where we are still and calm, such as playing the guitar, art or yoga (swan) or even lying on the lounge in complete relaxation (sloth). Too much time in sloth is terrible, too. A friend of mine made his fortune early and fulfilled his dream of retiring before 30 years of age. Initially he was elated and happy; however, the passion to play golf every day soon wore off. What I noticed was that his quality of life dropped dramatically. He had achieved all the goals he ever had, so his tiger and swan energies disappeared. I didn't see his happiness return until he sunk his teeth into his next passion.

In 2008 a study was published in *The Economic Journal* which showed that people's well-being improved more quickly after the death of their spouse than after one year of unemployment.[1] When I first read this, I didn't think it could be true. You are probably reading this thinking, it depends on the spouse. But the research seemed very sound and used a large sample size. When I reflected on it, it makes sense. A year of unemployment can involve a year of being bored, lacking goals, feeling as though you are not contributing, and lacking of identity. It would be incredibly devastating to anyone. It's a year of existing in sloth energy, which explains why a year of unemployment takes so long to recover from.

To some of you, the different energies might sound like mumbo jumbo; however, what I love about this concept is how practical and tangible it is. We can all relate to the different states and their simplicity allows us to apply it on a practical level.

So how exactly do we do that?

For most of us, it's pretty easy to do sloth energy. It doesn't require much training.

Step 1 – Locate lounge.

Step 2 – Assume the position and stay there.

In addition, I find that people don't have a problem getting into tiger energy as modern workloads force us into this energy state.

Let's focus on how we can embrace swan energy in the Rest phase of the Third Space. Small moments of swan energy in our day may not seem much on their own, but when you add them up over the day they mean a whole lot. Remember the elite tennis players in Chapter 2, who, between each point, calmed their physiology right down? While it may not have made a difference over one game, after three sets it starts to add up.

GO BACK TO SCHOOL

Having just got off a plane and battled the Friday afternoon Sydney traffic, I rushed into the John Colet School for my meeting with their principal, Gilbert Mane. I was greeted by a warm face and an even warmer disposition. Gilbert is the type of man you would want as your uncle, or would at least be happy to sit next to on a long flight. I was there because their bursar (the school's finance manager) had seen me present at a conference and talked to me afterwards.

'I love your Third Space concept. We do that at our school.' She immediately had my attention. 'What do you mean?'

She replied, 'Between every activity the kids do, they have a pause where they are still and then think about what they are about to transition into.' To say I was excited was an understatement. I had never thought about using the Third Space in schools.

When I sat down with Gilbert I outlined the concept of the Third Space and gave him the background. He immediately sat up straight in his chair and said, 'Yes, we absolutely incorporate the Third Space into the students' day.' I asked for details. He confirmed what the bursar had told me about the pauses between activities. 'Well, the children sit still in their chairs (being children, this is no mean feat), close their eyes and become present. They say a short mantra in Sanskrit and then they have to think about the next activity they are transitioning into. The reason they do this is to create a space between activities, to cut the tiger energy with swan energy. You could cut it with sloth energy, which obviously would rest their bodies, but the point of this activity is to be still yet aware. They are thinking about what they have just done and what they are about to transition into.' Gilbert believes that breaking this rest into short periods is a brilliant strategy. Over the course of the day the kids practise stillness ten to 12 times. In addition to this, those over ten years of age meditate for around five minutes each morning and afternoon within class. Over the course of a week this amounts to a large period of time where they are still yet alert; this is a great skill for children to have. Gilbert added, 'We see that this habit of pausing in the gaps as well as doing formal meditation leads to them being able to do tasks in a still but alert state. Our vision for the children is to have them totally immersed and present in life.'

Following our conversation, I did a tour of the school and went into the different classrooms. It's hard to describe but each classroom had a different energy to any other school I have been in. There was a calm but vibrant feel to each room, a sense of focus that most classrooms do not have. It was quite something. I watched the classes practise their stillness as they transitioned into their next lesson. The pause only lasts for a couple of moments but it is definite and significant. I kept saying to myself, 'I have to send my kids here.'

What is the result? John Colet is an incredibly successful school in an academic sense. They came fourth in the NAPLAN test (a nationwide test to determine the competence of the students) and many of their students receive scholarships for high school. In addition, they do extraordinary things that other schools do not; for example, each year the students perform a Shakespeare play and they also learn Sanskrit. So while the kids do well academically, they are exceptional at 'being on task' (focused and paying attention). For most children, it's rare to be focused for the majority of a 40-minute lesson. From my observation, the children at John Colet appeared to be far more on task than the average child. New teachers at the school comment on the fact that the children are so focused in class. Children who come to the school in the higher grades go home exhausted because they are trying to match the students who are already so good at staying focused.

Examining this case study, it's hard to determine causality and say that this Third Space-like transition is the reason for their development; however, you would have to be hard-pressed not to see the obvious link.

The John Colet case study illustrates the importance of the Rest phase in the Third Space. For all of us, the importance of Rest is that it cuts the tiger energy. If you live completely in tiger energy it will burn you out fast; it's like having the tiger by the tail. A great strategy for preventing burnout is to intersperse your day with swan energy. Unfortunately, many of us do not see the value of these regular, short, consistent moments of stillness.

CALL THE DOCTOR

Further evidence for the importance of Rest sporadically dropped into our day was presented to me when I met Craig Hassed, senior lecturer at the Monash University Department of General Practice. I had been asked to present to a group of general practitioners in the Hunter Valley. Following my presentation, I decided to hang around for lunch and the afternoon session. The afternoon session was titled 'Mindfulness', and was presented by Craig. As he started to present, what struck me was his amazing presence. He was incredibly calm and centred. Craig looked like a yoga master who had been dragged through an Armani store. I was mesmerised by his presentation and his ability to blend the scientific world and the ancient concept of mindfulness (where you are in the moment, otherwise called a state of swan energy). It was one of the most powerful presentations I had seen in years. In it, he talked about a study he had just completed where he looked at the impact of mindfulness on the well-being of medical students.

It is universally known that medical students commonly have terrible emotional well-being, due to their excessive workloads, their obsessional tendencies and high levels of stress. Research out of Duke University Medical School has shown that the rate of depression in undergraduate medical students is as high as 20 per cent.[2] Just as concerning is the fact that around 45 per cent of students self-medicate with alcohol and many use illicit drugs.[3]

Throw into this mix the fact that they are sleep deprived – which is another risk factor for depression – and you have yourself a group that is severely lacking in physical and psychological wellbeing. Ironic, considering they are learning how to *improve* people's health status. There is evidence to also suggest that an unhealthy doctor makes more mistakes, which is obviously not good for their patients. In one study it was found that depressed doctors made more than six times as many medication and prescribing errors.[4]

The poor well-being of the medical students was not lost on Craig and his colleagues. In response, Monash introduced the first mindfulness-based program to be integrated into the students' curriculum. It was called the Health Enhancement Program (HEP) and it is based on the Essence model.[5] In particular, the program heavily focused on the students practising mindfulness. All students were encouraged to introduce mindfulness into their lives in two ways.

1. *Practise mindfulness during daily tasks.* This consisted of them being present and mindful as they moved through their day, focusing on being in each moment and not focusing on the past or future.

2. *Formal mindfulness meditation practice.* Students were asked to do two five-minute 'full stops' in their day and as many 15–30-second 'commas'

as needed. In both cases they paused for that period of time, focused on their breathing, and were still.

The HEP was introduced halfway through their first semester and lasted for six weeks. At the beginning of the program the students had their physical and psychological well-being measured. At the conclusion of the program – which falls in exam week – their physical and psychological well-being was remeasured. Anyone that has been to university would know that exam week consists of four things: massive amounts of stress, a boatload of coffee, no sleep and more crying than a reality cooking show.

Considering they were retested in exam week, if their physical and psychological well-being remained steady it would have been a huge achievement. The HEP went way beyond that. At the end of the program the students reported a significant improvement in physical and psychological well-being. Their levels of depression, anxiety and hostility dropped by around 17 per cent. This was an amazing result and shows the benefits of these mindful pauses that we can take in our day.[6]

Surely if the concept of rest can work for a bunch of stressed-out, sleep-deprived medical students, it can help all of us to improve our physical and psychological well-being.

Resting in the Third Space may seem trivial on its own, but as a regular practice it has great power.

IMPROVING PERFORMANCE

The Rest portion of the Third Space can also improve our performance. In 1998, Linda Stone coined a phrase called 'Continuous Partial Attention (CPA)'. As the term implies, it is a state in which we are paying superficial attention to a number of things but not truly focusing on anything. Unfortunately, this is becoming our normal state. The majority of us are never truly 'present' with anything we do. Think about it. Do you ever have a conversation with someone who is physically there but you can tell that mentally they are somewhere else? Have you ever been on the phone with someone and heard computer keys tapping in the background, or pages turning? They are working while they are talking to you. Have you ever been on the phone to someone while you were working? You push the keys down softly so they can't hear you working.

Edward M. Hallowell, in his *Harvard Business Review* article 'Overloaded Circuits: Why Smart People Underperform', discussed a term called Attention Deficit Trait (ADT). This is where an adult's brain, during the work day, mimics that of a child with ADD. The adult doesn't actually have ADD but his or her brain acts like it does while at work. Someone with ADT has difficulty staying on task, can't focus, doesn't prioritise tasks, and starts a lot of things but completes very few of them. ADT is very similar to CPA and it simply means that a person's brain is conditioned to jump around and rarely focus on one thing.

The question is, why are we developing these conditions?

- *Gadget alert:* The introduction of new technology, such as instant messenger, email and smartphones, means that we are easily contacted or, more accurately, easily interrupted. The average office employee is interrupted every five and a half minutes. Around 28 per cent of the average person's day is lost due to distractions. Almost a third of a person's day is spent thinking, 'Now what was I just doing...?'

- *Space saver:* The cost of office space has made the open-plan office more popular; the result is a lack of privacy and distractions all around us.

- *Working in a vice:* The world has become condensed. Everyone wants something and they want it now. The business world has developed a sense of urgency about all tasks, even ones that aren't important. Because everything seems so urgent, we find ourselves constantly having to drop everything to suit other people's needs. Once, I was presenting to an IT company and we were discussing this issue when one man in the group started to laugh. I asked him what he was laughing about. He said, 'I just realised what I did yesterday. I sent someone internal an email. He didn't respond in 30 minutes so I sent him a text. He didn't reply to that so I called his mobile. He didn't answer that so I called his land line. He didn't pick up so I called the guy who sat next to him to find out where he was. He didn't know, so I went looking for him. I found him ... and I forgot what I wanted!'

- *Cultural resistance:* There is an attitude prevalent these days that if you close your office door, or tell people to come back another time, or tell them to leave you alone for the next two hours because you're trying to get something done, you're mean-spirited and not a team player.

- *Multi-tasking myth:* For too long people have prided themselves on multi-tasking. You often hear, 'You're a champion if you can multi-task' or, 'To do this role effectively you need to be a multi-tasker.' In theory, we're saying that we are focusing on two things at the one time. Impossible! The brain cannot consciously focus on two things that require attention at one time. What you're really doing is swap-tasking – swapping your focus from one task to another very quickly. Multi-tasking re-trains the brain to be scattered and jumpy.

Being under the influence of either ADT or CPA for too long has two big fallouts: it reduces our performance and it impacts on the quality of our relationships.

In January 2011, the state of New York introduced a bill that aimed to ban pedestrians from using their phone while crossing the street.[7] In the United States, researches at Ohio State University claim that the number of people admitted to hospital for mobile phone injuries is doubling every year.[8] Those people had, quite simply, been distracted while using their phone and either walked into something or fell over. Others have reported near misses such as walking in front of a car; one young man broke his nose by walking into a telegraph pole while texting a girl he was flirting with. This type of accident has become so common in London that some of the streets have become 'text safe': the lampposts are now padded to protect the wandering mobile phone user.[9]

PERFORMANCE

The brain is an incredibly complicated piece of machinery and in recent times the development of new technology has allowed us to gain a greater understanding of the brain. You can very crudely divide the brain into two main areas. There is the more cognitive/sophisticated part of the brain which helps us with recalling, organising and processing information, also called the neocortex. If you have ever looked at a picture of a brain, it's the wriggly bit on top. Below that, you have the more primitive part of the brain which is about emotion, the 'fight or flight' response, sexual desire, regulation of sleep and hunger. It reminds you to breathe and regulates things like your blood pressure and hormones. To be at your best you want the sophisticated part of your brain to be in control, and the primitive part to be backing it up without getting in the way. In particular, you want the frontal lobes (located behind your forehead) to run your day as this is the region in charge of high-level decision-making, organisation, prioritisation, predicting the future, creative thinking and innovation. This part of the brain also controls impulsive behaviour. When someone in the office annoys you, the primitive part of the brain says, 'Throw that stapler at their head,' while the frontal lobes chime in and say, 'Slow down cowboy, put the stapler away. Physical violence is not a good idea.'

What we are now discovering about the brain is that when the sophisticated frontal lobes have lots of information coming at them, or when they have to switch attention across a number of tasks, this region overloads and panics. At this point, it sends a stress response to the primitive part of the brain saying, 'We're freaking out. We are overwhelmed, we feel out of control and we doubt our ability to cope.' The primitive part of the brain says, 'Stress and fear? That's my job. I am taking over.' At this point, the sophisticated part of the brain goes quiet and the primitive part kicks into high gear. This is where you send emails you wish you could take back, or say things to people you didn't really mean.

The same thing happens when you have an argument. You are arguing over an issue and you start to get angry and flustered. The voice in the back of your head says, 'Come up with one good line that will just smash them.' But you're only coming up with terrible comebacks. You can't think of anything good to say. Why? The creative parts of the brain have been shut down and the primitive parts of the brain have kicked in. Twenty minutes after the argument ends, you suddenly think of all the things you should have said when the moment was there. You might think it's almost worthwhile calling them and restarting the argument just to get that final zinger in. Why do you think of something good to say when it's too late? You have calmed down, you're relaxed and the creative part of your brain has kicked back in.

The problem is that the primitive part of the brain is not very logical. It's impulsive and rash. You were once a teenager. Is the behaviour of teenagers challenging? You bet! They are selfish and do stupid things all the time. In a teenager, the connection between the frontal lobes and the primitive part of the brain is not fully developed. This means that a teenager's frontal lobes do not have good control over the primitive brain. ADT and CPA can shut down your frontal lobes and lead to your brain behaving like a teenager. Regularly and consistently slipping into Rest will calm and focus the brain.

In her book 'Choke', Sian Beilock talks about the merit of having a short pause before you take on a complex task or after you finish a task and tackle the next task.[10] The reason is that a short pause allows the frontal lobe to reboot itself and clear out unnecessary information. In addition, the frontal lobe simply gets fatigued, especially when you are doing cognitively stressful tasks. The pause allows the brain to recover some valuable nutrients to return it back to a high level of function.

When we experience a stressful event, the brain goes into a state of 'fight or flight' and prepares to fight or flee to ensure its survival. It shuts down the creative, innovative and highly cognitive parts of the brain in favour of the more primitive parts. This neurological change makes it almost impossible to perform at our best. However, research suggests that this 'performance shutdown' may last long after the stress has been removed. Dr Jiongjiong Wang from UCLA has shown that following a stressful event you are cognitively stunted beyond the removal of stress.[11] This is why it is crucial to have a Third Space with an effective Rest period following a stressful event to facilitate your brain returning to its best.

FACILITATING CREATIVITY

This frantic brain activity sees a huge reduction in creativity and innovation. A current trend I've noticed in business is that companies have shifted the focus away from 'How do we keep doing what we are doing and encourage company growth?' to 'How do we innovate and offer something truly unique?' Because of this trend, everyone is talking about innovation. A number of companies have asked me to present to their teams about how they can innovate more and stand out from the competition. What I find is that they are asking the wrong question. The question is not, 'What do we need to do to innovate?' We need to be asking, 'Why aren't we innovating right now?'

There are two main reasons for this.

Firstly, people are so frantic and interrupted that they never get into the space to think. Urgency has become more important than quality and uniqueness. The result is that they schedule brainstorming activities which rarely result in true innovation. It's unusual for a group of people to come up with a groundbreaking idea. These usually come from an individual with the time and space to open their mind.

Secondly, many companies have a culture that destroys innovation. Working with over 100 companies each year, I see so many of them start down the innovation path. The result is that they come up with great, innovative ideas, only to see their efforts fail from lack of follow-through. The research tells us that over 75 per cent of all change efforts fail. The reason: culture. For example, many companies have a culture where it is not okay to fail or look stupid. You cannot innovate in this environment.

Innovation relates to the Rest phase of the Third Space in that for innovation and creative thinking to happen, you need to have a calm, focused brain. While researching this book, I spoke to creative people in various fields – graphic designers, painters, songwriters, comedians and advertising executives. They each said they needed space, quiet and a still mind to innovate, and that the ADT or CPA mind kills innovation. Many people in creative roles said that in order to break down cross functional silos, their company decided to sit the creative people in the same space as process-driven people. The result was that the creatives hated it because the 'process people' often interrupted them with questions and comments.

We often hear stories from creatives in which their moments of inspiration hit them when they actually stopped thinking about the project and just let go. Great ideas would suddenly appear during these moments. This is because creativity often occurs in the Rest phase of the Third Space.

Steve Johnson, in his book *Where Good Ideas Come From: The Natural History of Innovation,*[12] says that the longer you can let an idea marinate, the more it evolves on a subconscious level. Ideas need time to incubate. When we run our ideas by others and allow them to influence our ideas, they evolve and gain form. The longer you can keep this part of the creative process going, the better the result, typically. This process relies heavily on large amounts of time for creativity to strike.

That is all well and good, but what if you're creative for a living? You may not have large amounts of time. If you are the creative director of an advertising agency you can't walk into a meeting with your best client and say, 'Yes, I know the outline was due today but I don't have anything for you – the inspiration just didn't hit me today. Sorry!' Fortunately, we can use the Third Space to actually drive and lead us into creativity.

Dan Gregory is the CEO of The Impossible Institute, an innovation and engagement organisation he founded after a 20-year career in advertising, which included the most successful new product launch in Australian history. In those 20 years he worked mostly in small entrepreneurial agencies as creative director. His job carries with it a huge number of micro-transitions. The challenge with smaller agencies is that you do not have a large amount of resources at your disposal, and so the delegation of tasks is severely limited. His day is not only about being creative but also selling to clients, meetings with stakeholders and managing other people in the organisation. Not only does Dan move between many tasks, he also needs to move between many different industries. Creative directors in large corporations may have only one big client to look after. However, the creative director in a small firm may have 20–30 clients from different industries, requiring them to bounce between half of them on any given day.

Dan has two big challenges in this role.

The first is finding how to be creative in an environment where he is constantly jumping between job roles, job tasks and industries.

The second is that deadlines and timelines in the advertising world have become obscenely short. In the past, you would have had three months to outline an idea and develop a campaign. Companies are now demanding this turnaround in one week.

When I sat down with Dan, he immediately related to using the Third Space to facilitate creativity.

'I definitely use this to transition into my creative space. I call it decompressing. I need to decompress out of a process mindset before I can become creative. I need to let go of what I have done before and become completely present, quiet and still. People make the mistake of thinking that creative departments are noisy and loud. It's the opposite: they are like libraries. In the past, I've worked for agencies where my role as creative director has seen me just attend meetings all day, which doesn't allow me a lot of space for innovation. When I raised this concern with managers they would say, "You get a 30-minute break between meetings. Can't you do it then?" While 30 minutes may be enough time to write it, it is not enough time to *not* be writing it. A non-creative liner job is easier to transition between; right now I have to write an email and ask that person for that report, then I need to generate an invoice for someone else, etc. These types of roles are easier to move between, but when high-level cognition and innovation are involved, the transitions are much harder. If my job is to try and convince 20 million Australians with the best drinking water on the planet that they need to pay more for water than petrol, that requires a level of sophistication and creativity beyond simple process. If I need to do four hours of creative work, it may take me 20 hours because of the transition time I need to get back into the right mindset.'

What I learned from Dan was that we need to transition into creativity; we can't just suddenly switch on the creative light. We need to decompress and facilitate the creative mind, and the key step here is to allow the moment of rest that calms the mind and allows it to be present and open to creativity. Rest is the prelude to creativity.

Because Dan is paid to be creative, he actively pushes himself into a creative space. His method is to segment his day into blocks of time where he can focus solely on creative ideas and innovation.

'If I'm in a creative space and someone comes up and asks me a question about an invoice for a client, I will actually yell at them. The reason is that once I transition out of that creative part of my brain it is very hard to move back. I find the transition from creative to cognitive very difficult and I have to protect it. I get up at 4am and do my creative thinking then, before anyone can screw my day up.

'You need to realise that creativity is a numbers game,' Dan said. I asked him how so.

He replied, 'If I asked a bunch of people who were untrained in writing ads to write an ad for Mercedes-Benz, they will all come up with the same ad. This is because they will only present their first thought. What you have to do is go through all the usual crap people think of before you can come up with something that is unexpected and new. That's how it's a numbers game. The process of writing the ad does not take time. What takes time is the process of dismissal of ideas that are too obvious and that the world has seen before.'

Dan's creative process is actually very structured and systematic. He will write for an hour with no expectation; he just throws down ideas without expecting that they are going to be the final idea. Another method he learned came from advertising icon Siimon Reynolds. You draw 20 boxes on a page and then write an idea in each box, not stopping until you have filled the entire page. What's important here is that there is no attachment to it. You aren't judging the ideas, but just letting them flow.

Regularly stepping into the Rest phase of the Third Space retrains your brain to focus and be still, allowing you to perform better and be more creative.

Another important reason for the Rest phase is the impact it has on the quality of our relationships.

RELATIONSHIPS NEED STILLNESS

I was driving along listening to a radio show about the recently deceased CEO of Apple, Steve Jobs. The conversation focused on what his legacy would be: would he be remembered as the man who changed the way we look at the world, or the man who destroyed personal relationships? As an Apple user, I thought the last statement was outrageous. Then I happened to turn to the car next to me. There was a mother and father in the front and two children in the back. They were each wearing iPod earphones, listening to different things, and clearly not talking to each other. In the following weeks I saw countless examples of this lack of connection. I once noticed a young couple in a fine dining restaurant who spent the entire meal on their iPhones without talking to each other.

It seems that we have lost the ability to sit, be still and live in the moment. As a presenter, I've noticed the attention spans of people getting worse over the years and I have purposefully changed my style of presenting to cope with this. I build in more stories, humour and interaction to keep them engaged. Phones are often a distraction, especially during workshops. People are constantly checking their phones, texting or sending emails. I presented at a conference once with Dr Thomas Frey, one of the world's top futurists, who told us that the average person pulls out their smartphone to check it every five minutes. Not long after that, I was presenting at another conference and decided to check out an earlier session to see what they were covering and how I could tie it to my own presentation. The morning presenter asked everyone to hand in their phones. About 45 minutes into it, you could see people start to squirm and fidget. They had separation anxiety from being away from their phones. At the 90-minute mark, one of the men in the group said, 'This is ridiculous. I want my phone back and I want it now.'

You often hear that great leaders have the ability to make you feel special. When they talk to you, you feel like the only person in the room. The ability to be present with another human being is an incredibly important skill to possess. When you are present with someone, it dramatically increases the level of trust and rapport that person feels for you.

Studies show that when managers are not present with their team members, a team member can walk away feeling unappreciated and may become disengaged. However, if the manager is truly present in the interaction, the team member will walk away with a sense of connection ('they heard me and they care') and is likely to be much more engaged. In particular, Tom Rath's findings from the research organisation Gallup, which specifically conducts research into workplace engagement and performance, have shown that if you have a manager who is ignoring you and not being present when you interact, your chance of being actively disengaged increases by 40 per cent. In contrast, if you have a manager who is critical of you but pays you attention and is present during the interaction, your chance of becoming actively disengaged drops to around 22 per cent. What this tells us is that you don't even have to be nice to people; as long as you are present with them, you can increase their level of engagement. However, the study showed that when mangers were present with team members and focused on their strengths, what they are doing well and what they are achieving, their chance of being disengaged was only one in 100.[13]

I was once at a conference with one of the world's leading experts on the cognitive development of children. At the time, my wife Chris was 36 weeks pregnant. I found the expert in the speakers' room and accosted him.

'I'm about to have a baby and everything I read is telling me to do something different. It seems that you can mess your kids up really easily. Help me! What are the most important things I need to do to raise a happy child?'

He laughed and said, 'Just relax and try not to believe everything you read. There are four big things you need to do. Number one, talk to them as much as possible. We have found a correlation between the number of words said to a child each day and their cognitive development.

'Number two, don't label them. Never call them "bad boy" or "bad girl" or "good boy" or "good girl". You don't want them associating their self-worth with the things they do. They need to know that you love them regardless of what they do. They don't have to do things to be good – they are inherently good. When they misbehave, focus on the behaviour: "That behaviour is inappropriate," or "You cannot do that," rather than "You are a bad boy."

'Thirdly, as early as possible teach them empathy. When they do something to another child (such as push them or take their toy), ask your child to think about how they might have made the other child feel.

'Finally, when you interact with them be present. The human face stimulates more brain activity than anything else. So when a child is looking at a human face, his or her brain activity is at its highest point. When the person they are looking at is deeply present, brain activity increases even more. For a child's brain to develop well, that child needs interactions with people who are completely present with them. Be present with your child as much as possible.'

I was once presenting to a group of sewage treatment workers. I had two full days with the group. We finished the first day talking about being present specifically in an occupational health and safety context. As I stood up to kick off day two, I was interrupted by a man in the front row. His name was Mark Hunter. Mark was a tattooed, hairy, nuggety, foul-mouthed Aussie bloke (you're probably thinking, as opposed to all those gentle, feminine men who work at the sewage treatment plant). As I was about to start, Mark interrupted me.

'Hey, Ads,' he said. 'I went home last night and was just watching the telly, lying on the lounge minding my own business. Then all of a sudden the wife comes in and starts nagging me. She is banging on about something, I don't know what. I hear your voice in my head saying, "Be present, Mark." I turned to her and said, "Hang on", turned the TV off, turned back to her and said "What's up love?" She almost fell over. Then this morning I'm eating me breakfast and I always read the paper while I eat me breakfast. The wife sits down across the table from me. Once again I hear your bloody voice in my head saying, "Be present, Mark." So I fold the paper over and I push it aside and look at her ... I haven't looked at her in years. She is bloody beautiful.'

Matthew Killingsworth, a doctoral student in psychology at Harvard University, has shown that 46.9 per cent of our day is spent in a non-present state. For almost half of our day, our minds are wandering somewhere else. When we have a wandering mind, our productivity really suffers. 'Of course it does,' I hear you say. However, where his research really becomes interesting is that when our minds wander, we experience our greatest moments of unhappiness. Why? Because this is when the mind invariably drifts into personal concern. In contrast, Killingsworth found that our greatest moments of happiness are when our minds are present and immersed in a task. A focused brain is one that doesn't have the time or space for worry and stress.[14]

We can all benefit from the increase in focus and ability to be present that the Rest phase of the Third Space can bring. Regularly practising the Rest phase:
- improves our ability to be still and focused
- improves performance and productivity
- facilitates creativity and innovation
- reduces our chance of burnout

- improves relationships.

HOW TO MOVE INTO REST

There are two main focuses of the Rest phase.

First, slow down your breathing so that you have long, slow, controlled breaths. Our breathing pattern is our built-in relaxation switch. Our nervous systems and the chemical status of our bodies are greatly affected by our breathing patterns. At a basic level, you have two sides to your nervous system: the sympathetic nervous system, which speeds you up (triggered by the 'fight or flight' response, this gets you ready for action) and the parasympathetic nervous system, which slows everything down and makes you feel calm and relaxed. When you breathe rapidly and shallowly you engage your sympathetic nervous system. When you breathe slowly and deeply you engage your parasympathetic. Whenever you enter Rest, ensure that you slow down your breathing. It's like pressing pause on the remote that controls your nervous system. The time sequence for breathing will vary between people, but a general guide is to breathe in for four counts, hold for two counts and breathe out for six counts.

Second, focus your mind on the present moment. If you are sitting on a chair, pay attention to how the chair feels against your body – every detail, every touch point. Or if you are looking at something, once again, focus on every detail of it. Be completely present with that image.

If the Rest period extends beyond a minute, you may want to introduce various relaxation techniques to keep your mind focused on the present moment. Here are some ideas:

- Focus on your breathing: count along with your breathing, counting as you breathe in, as you hold it and as you breathe out. You can also focus on the temperature difference between the air you breathe in and the air you breathe out (air in is cooler than air out). One of my personal favourites is to focus on breathing in up the left nostril, breathing out down the right nostril, then breathing in up the right nostril and out down the left nostril. Repeat this pattern. Now, of course you can't do it, but trying to do it focuses the mind.

- You can focus on tensing and relaxing different parts of your body. For example, tense and curl up your toes, then relax them. Do the same with your calf muscles. Keep going until you have gone through all the different muscles in your body.

- Repeat a mantra. As you are breathing slowly, you can focus on the words or the sound of a mantra. In its basic form you can repeat a phrase like 'I am calm' or 'I am present now', and concentrate on the words to keep your mind focused. Some people make the 'Om' sound. Really, it's about whatever you feel comfortable with.

Consistent practice of the Rest phase leads to a more calm and focused mind, lower stress levels and an ability to be present. Practise it on a regular basis and you will move into the next space with a clearer mind and a calmer manner. It will also reduce the impact of each transition by reducing your stress levels and maintaining your energy levels.

SUMMARY

- The Rest phase is where we take a moment to pause, calm our minds and be present in the moment. It may be as short as a few seconds or, if life permits, significantly longer. It centres us so that we can move onto the last phase of the Third Space – Reset.
- Regular practice of Rest retrains our brains to be calm and focused. It also brings with it the following benefits:

  –It improves performance and productivity

  –It facilitates creativity and innovation

  –It reduces our chance of burnout by reducing our stress levels

  –It improves relationships by allowing us to connect and be in the moment.

Chapter 8

How will I 'show up'? – Reset

Now we move into the final phase of the Third Space: Reset. This is where you prepare yourself for the Second Space you are transitioning into. Reset is where you focus on that next space and think about what you want to achieve. You use this phase to develop awareness of your current behaviour and concentrate on the behaviour you want to exhibit in that next space. In other words, Reset is all about thinking, 'When I get to the Second Space, how will I "show up"?'

HAPPY CAMPER

When I was 21, I stopped being a self-centred 'all the world revolves around my hindquarters' post-teenager and discovered that there were other people on this planet. I developed a desire to contribute to something bigger than me. The search began for a project to vent my new-found benevolence. It ended with a charity called Camp Quality. Camp Quality is a charity for children with cancer, which supports not only the children but also their families. Twice a year, they take children with cancer away for a week-long camp, where they forget their troubles and have a heck of a good time. When I joined the organisation, my role was as a companion. As a companion, your job is to attend the camps and look after a camper. Unless there are any specific problems, you're usually with the same camper for the time that you are involved with the organisation.

My first camp was also the first for my four-year-old camper, Christopher. Christopher was an old, gentle soul. You know, those smiling patient kids who seem like a tiny version of Mr Miyagi from *The Karate Kid.* He was in remission from a brain tumour and his operation had not only scarred his skull, but his body as well. During one of his many operations, the part of his brain responsible for co-ordination and body movement had been damaged. Christopher walked like an old man and when he tried to run it looked like his limbs were moving to their own and very different beat. What he lacked in physical attributes he made up for in kindness and beauty of spirit. Christopher was the most considerate child I have ever met, who always put other people's needs before his. He also had a wicked sense of humour and every day had a new joke. His favourite was, 'How do you make a dog meow? Put it in a freezer for a week and run it through a bandsaw. Me-owwwwwwwwwwww!'

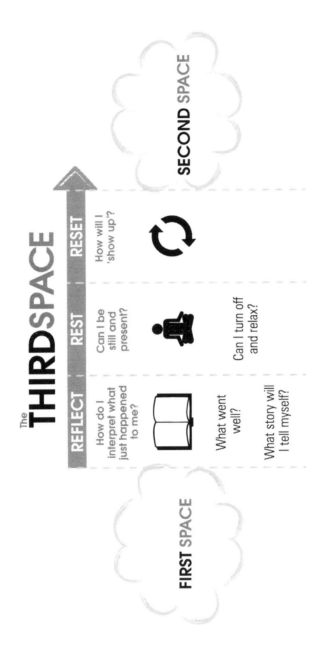

On one particular camp, we were sharing a room with another companion, Travis, and his camper, Cameron. Two days into the camp, Travis became sick and had to go home. The duty to look after Cameron fell to me. Cameron had also had a brain tumour and was the same age as Christopher.

Cameron oozed personality and seemed far older than his small size would give him credit for. He had a shock of white hair on his head and pale blue eyes. The statements he would come out with cracked me up. When I asked him what he wanted to do when he grew up, expecting the usual response of pilot or fireman, he told me he planned to 'own a number of KFC franchises and then sink the profits in to real estate and retire young'. His mother once told me that his older brother and younger sister wanted a raise in their pocket money. When Cameron negotiated the deal with his parents, he also negotiated a 40 per cent rise, indexed to inflation, but kept 30 per cent for himself. He certainly was a character and, like Christopher, his gentleness and generosity humbled me.

When Cameron had to go to hospital for treatment (which was a lot), he would drag all the toys out of his room into the lounge room, divide them into piles and place a name next to each pile. He was thinking that if he wasn't able to enjoy them, at least his friends should. Doctors that treated him commented to me how unselfish he was – the whole time he was in hospital he was concerned with the well-being of other children in the hospital, asking how they were and if there was anything he could do for them.

Over the years I grew closer to both boys, often seeing them outside of camp.

In December I received a devastating phone call. I was told that Cameron had relapsed and was back in hospital. Two days later, while still regaining my breath from the first body blow, I was told that Christopher's tumour had relapsed and was unbelievably aggressive. When I turned up at his house, Christopher had slipped into a coma and was not expected to ever regain consciousness. He looked like he was only asleep and seemed comfortable and at peace. Cameron, on the other hand, was not battling cancer but a serious chest infection that he had picked up in hospital.

Upon arriving at Cameron's house I was traumatised by what I found. He was lying on the lounge with an oxygen mask over his face. Gone was the milk white hair, blue eyes and pale complexion; they had been replaced by an emaciated, tiny little body and a bald head that looked like a jigsaw puzzle after multiple head operations. At one point during the visit, his oxygen bottle ran out and I watched him panic and gasp for air as his mother quickly changed the mask to a fresh bottle.

In January, Christopher and Cameron passed away, 17 hours apart. Christopher never regained consciousness and slipped away peacefully in his sleep. Cameron, on the other hand, was as polite in death as he was in life. While lying on the lounge breathing in his oxygen, he pulled the mask off his face, looked his mum in the eye and said, 'I can't do it anymore. I can't fight. Would it be okay if I gave up?', to which his mother said, 'It's okay baby.' Cameron died moments later.

His funeral was on a Tuesday in January in a small, regional town in NSW. When I turned up to the funeral the entire town was there and a heavy sense of grief filled the air. I have never seen sadness like it. The day before his funeral it had been brutally hot, which was normal for that time of year. But on the day of Cameron's funeral, it was bitterly cold, raining and windy. It was almost as if the weather was sharing our grief. Nothing could prepare me for the pure sadness that seemed to leach out of me. It was unbearable. I was sad for his family but most of all I was sad because the world was a poorer place for his passing.

The following day was Chris's funeral, at which I was asked to speak. As a professional speaker, it was the hardest presentation I have ever had to do.

Right then, every pathetic, self-indulgent moment of my life flashed before my eyes. I thought of the months spent pining over broken relationships, so many wasted hours being angry over something insignificant, stressing over events that turned out to be nowhere near as devastating as my overactive mind had anticipated. I walked away from this period of my life thinking that from now on, I was going to be different. An experience as profound as this would surely change me. For a time, it was true. After the funerals I stressed less, appreciated my friends more and held my loved ones more often and a little tighter. But it didn't last. I began to fall back into my old patterns. After a bad day I would take it out on the people around me, I would be precious about little setbacks and, quite simply, I would be a drama queen. The effect of Cameron and Christopher wore off. It's like being inspired by an uplifting movie. It lasts for a couple of days, and then you go back to your normal set point. Changing habits and improving behaviour is a choice. You must choose to show up with this new behaviour every day. What Christopher and Cameron taught me is that in order to be more grateful and happier in each moment I had to choose to be more grateful and happier in each space I moved into.

One of the great things about marrying someone far brighter than you is that you are constantly learning. On our honeymoon I asked my wife if she had any ideas on how we could make our marriage work. She replied, 'Being married is a choice. For a marriage to last you must wake up each day and say, "I choose to be married and I use today to improve the relationship."' I thought, wow, I married Buddha.

I wake up at 5.30 every morning to exercise and it's a struggle every time. I find myself regularly doing maths in the morning. You know what I'm talking about. The alarm goes off at 6am. You roll over, hit snooze and go back to sleep. Alarm goes off again, you roll over, hit snooze and ... you go back to sleep. Alarm goes off a third time, you hit snooze again, but instead of going back to sleep you shift into mathematician mode. This is where you lie in bed and actually calculate in your head the latest time you absolutely, positively, have to get out of bed. It goes like this: 'Okay, I had a shower the day before last, so forget that. I don't need to brush my teeth because I have gum,' – you get the picture – and you come to the conclusion that in order to leave the house at 7am you can get up at 6.58am.

As much as I love exercise, I do maths every morning. I would rather lie in a nice, warm bed and cuddle up to my wife than go out in the freezing cold. To wake up at 5.30 every morning is a conscious choice. There was no magic switch flipped to suddenly make it easy. I have to choose to get out of bed every single time.

We rarely go through experiences that lead to lasting change. For these things to happen, we must 'show up' every time and choose this new behaviour in each space we move into. We use Reset to ensure that we show up at our best.

HOW DO WE CHOOSE TO 'SHOW UP' BETTER?

In June 2001, as a PhD student, I achieved one of my life's dreams, which was to present at the annual conference for the American College of Sports Medicine (ACSM), held, this particular year, in Baltimore. This conference is considered the holy grail of human sports performance. When I applied to give an oral presentation of my research, other PhD students laughed at me. They said, 'There is no way you will get an oral presentation. You may be allowed to put up a poster in the main hall, but there's no way you will get on the program. PhD students rarely get to present.' I ignored them and obsessed over the application. ACSM contacted me months later to inform me that I would be presenting my research in one of the main halls. I was ecstatic. This conference was like Disneyland for a performance nerd. All the greatest minds in sports performance in one room – and I got to meet all my heroes. Americans, being the warm, hospitable people that they are, invited me to their labs to hang out and learn how they do things in the US.

I spent the next three months on Greyhound buses and Amtrak trains travelling all over the US, sleeping on people's floors, and learning from their studies on improving human performance. I was lucky enough to meet a sports psychologist who had tested Tiger Woods. In 2001, Tiger Woods was in blistering form and dominating the game of golf. I said to this psychologist, 'What is it about Tiger that makes him so amazing?' His face lit up and he said, 'I have never been a cheerleader in my life but this guy just blows my mind. His ability to focus and be present with a task is unparalleled. He is so focused that when he lines up the shot he is actually disconnected from the outcome of the shot. Adam, the epitome of performance is the ability to perform a task and not worry about your performance or the outcome. Whether you're an ice hockey player faced with a shot at an open goal to win the championship, a basketball player taking a three-point shot with two seconds left on the board, or a baseball player going through a batting slump, disconnection is the key to performance and Tiger is a master at it.'

This conversation has stayed with me since. In the years following, I noticed that when people were able to disconnect from the outcome or the worry of doing a good job and simply focus on the task, their performance dramatically improved. This is the point of the Reset phase. As we transition into the Second Space, we become immersed in the task rather than worry about the outcome or our performance, whether it's a sales pitch, putting on a dinner party, an exam or asking someone out on a date. We use Reset not to worry about the outcome or performance, but to focus on the next space.

SHOW UP TO EACH SPACE WITHOUT DESPERATION

I found the best salespeople were those who picked up the phone, focused on the conversation and did not worry about the outcome. They weren't desperate or attached to making the sale. Heidi Gregory is one of the best salespeople and sales managers I have ever met. Heidi works for me and often has days where she makes 200 sales calls in a day. I once asked her how she managed to make such a large volume of calls. She said, 'I treat a call day like a game of golf. Each call is a different shot. Some shots go in the rough, others go on the green. When I have a bad call I just tell myself that one went in the water and I focus on the next one. In golf, you line up the shot and have a couple of practices. Before each call I make sure I'm clear on my intention and I do my research. You wouldn't walk off the course after one bad shot. Likewise, I don't drop my bundle after a couple of bad calls.'

I did a project with some musicians about getting into flow (that state where we are in the zone and perform at our best), and we found what facilitated flow was when they walked out on stage thinking, 'They either like it or they don't; either way I am good at what I do and I don't need their approval.' The best performers were the ones who didn't need or seek out the audience's approval: they were comfortable in their skin and confident in their ability.

When I decided I wanted to be a professional presenter, the very first presentation I designed was one on health. It started with ten stick figures on the board. I walked up to the board and said, 'If these ten people represent everyone in this room, this is how you are going to die. Three of you will die of cancer, four will die from heart disease, one will have an accident, one will die of a neurological disease...,' and so on. I kept going until they were all dead. I know – cheery stuff. I then went on to guilt the audience about how they don't prioritise their health and that it's because health is not a sign of success. Success for us comes from things like having a big house or a nice car. Our health doesn't really come into it. I continued, 'Well, while we're talking about success, let's look at the bell curve that outlines our definition of success throughout our lives.' The bell curve of success is an old joke that many speakers use when they present; in fact, I'm not even sure of its origin.

The bell curve starts when we are three, when success means not peeing our pants. At 17, success is having a driver's license.

At 20, success is having sex.

At 30, success is money.

At 40, success is money.

And at 50, success is also having money.

(Now, here comes the joke.)

At 70, success is having sex.

At 75, success is having a driver's license.

And at 80 (you guessed it), success is having not peed our pants.

That was the first five minutes of my presentation. Subtle, I know.

You wouldn't believe it though, I got a booking. I was asked by a Rotary Club in Western Sydney to come and present to them. I didn't know what a Rotary Club was.

I turned up with my flip chart and stick figures, I had my pens and I was ready to tell these people how it is and to get them healthy. I walked in.

Everyone in the room was close to or over the age of 80. What do I do? I thought.

The problem was that I only knew one presentation – the 'pee in your pants at 80' presentation – and I was about to speak to a group of 80-year-olds. I had no choice; I had to do the presentation. It was a disaster. They hated me: people left the room and one man in the front row turned his chair around to face the other way and started reading a book. I couldn't blame them. I'd shown up, told them how they were going to die and that it would be a miracle if they didn't wet themselves by the end of the presentation.

It was a traumatic experience. Because of this, for a period of time afterwards, I wanted – needed – my audience to like me and tell me that I was okay. I had an internal focus. All I thought about was whether they liked me or not. As I was presenting, I was saying to myself, 'What am I going to say next? Am I doing a good job? Does the audience like me, are they getting value from this?' This mindset drove me crazy because I judged my performance purely on the reaction of the group. The problem was that I was focusing on the only thing I couldn't control. You can control your performance, but you can't control whether the audience will like you. This is why a large percentage of the population rates public speaking as a greater fear than death. What do they fear? They fear judgement, they fear that a group of people will tell them that they are not okay. Bad presenters are the ones who look to the audience to validate them.

Because I had this mindset, my presenting suffered. Luckily, my speaking mentor Doug Malouf took me aside and said, 'Five per cent of your audience will hate you no matter what you do. They just won't like the way you look, talk or walk. You might remind them of someone they don't like or they're having a bad day and you'll cop it. Don't base your self-worth on what the audience thinks of you because it will drive you crazy.' When I really took this attitude on board and no longer needed the approval of the people in my audience, my presenting stepped up to a new level. In particular, what this did was free up my mental space to focus on mastering the presentation rather than obsess over whether they liked me or not.

The same thing happens in relationships. When you obsess over your partner and become needy, you become less attractive and they don't want you as much anymore. A healthy relationship is where each person loves each other without expectation. They focus on making the relationship as good as it can be rather than saying, 'I need you to love me and make me okay.'

THE HARDEST JOB IN THE WORLD

When I was writing this book, I tried to picture the most difficult job to 'show up' for. I thought brain surgeon, I thought police officer, I thought race car driver. I finally decided on what I consider to be the toughest job in the world. Stand-up comedian! This must be the toughest job ever. To stand up in a club filled with drunk people and make them laugh. The thought terrifies me, but I take my research seriously and so I signed up for a standup comedy course. It is by far the hardest thing I've ever done. You have to make your audience laugh at least every 20 seconds or you die. But once again, I noticed that the best people in the course were the ones who got up on stage and didn't care what the audience thought of them. They didn't need their approval. I went to comedy shows and watched professional comedians. What separated the good from the bad was a lack of neediness. It's funny: audiences are like packs of wild animals – they can smell neediness and fear a mile away. As soon as they get a sniff of it, the comedian is dead meat. When an audience knows that you need its laughter, it will never give it to you.

I interviewed a few comedians to find out how they disconnect and drop the need for approval.

One of them said that as he walks up on stage he says to himself over and over again, 'They laugh or they don't laugh, either way, f*@k them. I don't care what they think. I don't need them to tell me I'm okay!' A bit full on, don't you think? I asked him so.

'It has to be,' he replied. 'Stand-up is so challenging that you need to take your mindset to an extreme. It's easy to get attached to the outcome when you have 1000 people expecting you to make them laugh every 20 seconds. This statement gives me enough thrust to escape the gravity of attachment. This mantra helps me be attached to what I believe but detached from the outcome of it.' All the comedians that I talked to said a similar thing. The more detached they became from needing approval, the better their performance became. The more detached they became from approval, the more alignment there was between what they said on stage and what they passionately believed.

They used the Reset phase of the Third Space before they got on stage to squash any desperation and attachment they may have.

WHAT DRIVES US IN THE SECOND SPACE

Goal theory tells us that when we enter the Second Space we can approach the desire to perform from one of three main focuses.

EGO BOOST

This is where we are only interested in doing well so that our ego is inflated. We want to perform so that we get praise and recognition. Our only interest in the task is the adulation that we perceive to be on the other side. People with this focus believe that doing well is the key to their self-worth – 'If I achieve it, it shows me that I am smart, I am funny, I am capable, I am popular,' and so on.

An example of this is basketball player Scotty Pippen. At the end of the 1993–94 season, the Chicago Bulls (Pippen's team) were playing their rivals, the New York Knicks. They were down by two games and desperately needed to win. With 1.8 seconds left, the Bulls were losing by one point. Phil Jackson, the coach, had designed the play for Toni Kukoc to take the final shot. When he heard this, Pippen refused to go back in the game unless he took the final shot. He was focused on his own ego.

Ego is a dangerous driver because you can become discouraged when you get negative feedback. It makes you a non-team player, and when you start to lose or face adversity, you can fall apart. As well as that, people with this strong driver are more likely to cheat (as they will do anything to win), or rely on shallow improvement such as rote learning, rather than a deep understanding of the task. In an organisation, if you have a team with a lot of these people they will be disloyal to the rest of the team and sabotage others to get ahead.

AVOIDING FAILURE

This is where not failing, or not looking stupid, drives you. Your focus is on the fact that you do not want to look like an idiot. This is a disastrous driver because it gets you to focus on the negative things that could go wrong, puts you in a state of anxiety, and causes you to feel negative emotions such as fear or panic. Negative emotion reduces your performance and creativity.

You often see tennis players who are in a seemingly unbeatable position choke and fall apart. When the player realises they are 5-1 ahead in the final set their focus becomes, 'Don't lose this – you will look like an idiot if you lose this match from 5-1 in front. Do not screw up.' Once the player shifts into this pattern of thinking, their game starts to fall apart. Often in cricket you see batters go through a form slump where they can no longer score runs. A slump perpetuates itself because every time the batter gets to the crease s/he is thinking, 'Don't get out, don't get out. Your career will be over if you don't get some runs.' The player focuses on not failing.

MASTERY

This is where your entire personal drive is to improve your performance and complete the task in a better fashion. Your sense of satisfaction stems only from becoming more competent at what you are doing. In other words, you are driven by internal motivation, not external. You are not being influenced by external motivation like praise, scores or winning. Because of this, you are far more likely to consistently perform as you are not derailed by external factors. Having a mindset that is of this orientation is associated with high performance, deeper engagement with the task and greater perseverance in the face of setbacks.

One of the many benefits of focusing on mastery is that it's a state of high engagement and continual improvement. When I was at the Australian Institute of Sport I noticed that some of the most talented athletes never achieved their potential because success came easily to them. They never developed a strong work ethic and simply went through the motions at training. I also found that the athletes who had to work hard for success would eventually surpass the more talented athletes because of their commitment to mastery.

One man who got his team to focus on mastery is college basket ball coach John Wooden. John is one of the most successful basketball coaches in history and what made him unique is that he never talked to his team about winning or losing. His focus was getting them to master the game of basketball. His view was that if you focus on the metrics of the game, the result would take care of itself. He wanted each player to focus on specific aspects going into the game. For example, one player may focus on reducing turnovers, while another would focus on increasing the number of rebounds or increasing his court speed.

John once said that he knew he was a successful coach when his team left the dressing room and outsiders couldn't tell whether they'd won or lost – he made sure his team left the dressing room with the same attitude and emotions every time. Even if his team won, he might be disappointed in them if they did not improve in the metrics of the game. The whole focus was mastery.

When you 'show up', what drives you to succeed? Are you doing just enough so you don't run into trouble? Are you the type of person who only puts in a determined effort if you know it will further your career or earn you praise? Or do you 'show up' hoping to do things a little better every day?

It's imperative that when we 'show up' we are focusing on mastering whatever we are doing. Start to implement mastery into more parts of your life – at work, in personal relationships and with your passions. Mastery allows you to detach from worry about the outcome or your performance.

This concept of detachment is not about being cold, unfeeling or uncaring. It's about caring about the things you can control and doing the best job of that.

MASTERY AND ENGAGEMENT IS VITAL FOR WELL-BEING

HOW DO YOU 'SHOW UP' TO WORK?

How you 'show up' is important for your overall well-being. Let's look at the impact 'showing up' well in one part of your life can have on your life overall. Let's examine how you show up for work.

I believe that people chronically underestimate the impact their state at work has on their overall well-being. The majority of our time is spent at our place of work and we often spend our personal time talking about or thinking about work. People who enjoy their work are 200 per cent more likely to have thriving overall well-being.

According to research organisation Gallup, there are three types of employees:

Engaged: These people show up to work with enthusiasm and are constantly looking to improve their performance. They are driven by mastery, doing their job better today than they did it yesterday. They have a positive impact on work culture, move the organisation forward, and drive innovation.

Unengaged: These people show up to work neutral. They have 'checked out', so they do the job but don't have any enthusiasm, energy or passion in their work. They still get things done, but they are merely going through the motions. They tend not to become involved in trying to improve culture at the workplace.

Actively disengaged: These people have quit, but they haven't had the decency to resign. They don't like their job and actively look for trouble. They show up with negative emotion and often aim to do as little work as possible. They undermine the company and the engaged workers.

According to the Gallup Q12 Employee Engagement Poll (2008) results, only 18 per cent of workers in Australia are engaged. Sixty-one per cent of workers are unengaged and 21 per cent are actively disengaged.

In their book *Wellbeing – The Five Essential Elements,* Tom Rath and Jim Harter showed that people who were actively disengaged were almost 200 per cent more likely to develop depression than engaged employees. Why is there such a strong relationship? Engagement is beneficial for your mental health. When you are engaged, all you are thinking about is the present moment. You are paying attention to each detail and asking yourself, 'Can I do this better, faster, more efficiently?' Research by prominent psychologist Mihalyi Csikszentmihalyi found that people with chronic depression and eating disorders felt a predominance of negative emotions and negative self-talk. When given a task that they could completely engage in, their emotions and thoughts became indistinguishable from those of people without their conditions.[1] It's clear that being present with tasks is important for our mental and emotional wellbeing. Likewise, engagement affects our behaviour in the home. When interviewed, 54 per cent of actively disengaged employees said that work stress caused them to behave poorly with family or friends, while only 17 per cent of engaged employees reported that work stress had caused them to behave poorly in the home.[2]

An English study followed a group of healthy men over ten years.[3] The study found that male employees who had favourable perceptions of their work environment were 30 per cent less likely to suffer from coronary heart disease than male employees who had negative perceptions of their work environment. The findings remained consistent even when the researchers tested controlling factors such as age, ethnicity, marital status, educational attainment, socioeconomic position, cholesterol level, obesity, hypertension, smoking, alcohol consumption and physical activity. The study found that work attitude was the defining variable.

This lack of engagement also has a detrimental impact on a company's profits. Disengaged employees are more likely to steal from the company, have an accident, and be involved in bullying or harassing behaviours. Some studies have actually shown that you can correlate share price with the number of engaged employees you have.[4]

NO JOB IS BETTER THAN A BAD JOB

Earlier in this book, we talked about the fact that people recover quicker from the death of their spouse than a year of unemployment. Researchers at the Australian National University decided to examine the impact of having a job you did not enjoy (low levels of control, high demands and complexity, job insecurity and unfair pay) on your mental health compared to unemployment. They found that poor quality jobs led to larger declines in mental health than being unemployed.[5] What they showed was that the quality of your job predicts the quality of your mental health.

HOW WE 'SHOW UP' AFFECTS OTHERS

How you 'show up' (your emotional state, your mindset and your behaviour) for work has a huge impact on your well-being and performance. And if you are a leader or manager, the way you 'show up' will determine the mood and productivity of your team. The number one reason people give for leaving their last job is a poor relationship with their direct manager. Time and time again, research shows that the person we least like being around is our boss. Managers and leaders need to 'show up' better to engage their teams.

Caroline Bartel, Associate Professor at the University of Texas, and Richard Saavedra, Associate Professor at the University of New Hampshire, collaborated in 2000 to discover that people in meetings adopted the same mood within two hours.[6] They also found that teams of workers experienced the same emotions over the week, even though the individuals in those groups were varied in terms of external stress and challenges. What this shows is that we share emotions with the people around us. Think about it for a moment. Have you ever walked into a room and immediately felt the tension in the air? When you spend time with happy people, how do you feel? Happy! When you spend time with sad people how do you feel? Sad. As humans, we sense and share emotions from those around us. Going to watch a sporting event on your own in the stands is nowhere near as exciting as it is if you are surrounded by 80,000 people.

How does this happen? The scientific world is still debating this. Some believe that the 'mirror' brain cells that we have allow us to sense and adopt the mood of the people around us. This also makes evolutionary sense. If the people around you are feeling aggressive, you might need to know about it to stay alive, so sensing how people feel is an advantage. Beyond this, if you can sense how someone else feels, you can build rapport and a bond with them. If you have a bond you will form a tribe. If you are in a tribe, you will stay alive.

We each affect the mood and culture of our organisation. Having said that, the greatest influence on a team is the mood of the leader. It is so potent that many leaders should consider their primary task as the emotional leadership of their team.

Pause for a moment and consider how you might affect the mood of your team. This is not just about the leader. It drives me crazy when people say culture at work only comes from the top down. While it's heavily influenced by the people at the top, it also comes from the bottom up.

It's in our own interest to 'show up' well at work. Our mood affects the people around us and their mood affects us. If a direct social connection to you is happy, your chance of being happy increases by around 15.3 per cent. If a friend of a friend (someone you don't have direct contact with) is happy, the odds of you being happy increases by 9.8 per cent. If someone three degrees removed from you is happy, your chance of being happy goes up 5.6 per cent.[7]

To put this in context, a $10,000 pay rise is thought to lead to a 2 per cent increase in happiness.[8]

HOW TO BE ENGAGED YET DISCONNECTED FROM THE OUTCOME

One of the great Australian moments in the Sydney Olympics was when Kerri Pottharst and Natalie Cook won gold in the beach volleyball. The whole nation held its breath as the two battled it out against the Brazilian pair. The great thing about beach volleyball is the huge amount of micro-transitions made during the game. Every point is a new space that the player moves into. Each time that player transitions into a new point, she has to leave the previous point behind (regardless of whether she won or lost it) and clear her mind for the next point. I interviewed Kerri Pottharst to find out how she handled these micro-transitions on the court.

'Competition is very different to training. When I lose a point in competition I don't think about it at all because I don't have the time to fix it. At training, in between points I pause and learn from the shot and think about what I need to do differently. In competition, I can't do this. The focus is to get rid of the previous point. I may have a fleeting feeling of disappointment but I get rid of that as fast as possible. I have a routine for doing this. I would lift my sunglasses and run my finger across my eyebrows and flick the sweat off. As I did that, I visualised getting rid of any negative thoughts and emotion that I might take through to the next point.'

This is analogous to Reflect in the Third Space.

'Then I focus on preparing for the next point. When I'm serving, I go through a specific routine. I adjust my hat, I wipe my hands on the back of my swimmers to ensure they are dry, then get in my ready position. I get the ball off the ball person. I then slap the ball in between my hands and say the word 'ball' to myself, and then I look at my foot and say 'foot'. I then look at the opposition's line, as that is where I want the ball to land, and say 'line'. As I toss the ball in the air I say 'toss' and I hit the ball. The more distractions – like nerves, noise and weather – and pressure I am under, the more I use that routine.

'In the last two points of the gold medal match I used this routine and served my two hardest serves. The second-last serve was an ace and the last serve was one where their return went out. I was so focused in the last two moments of that match I felt like I was in a cocoon. I've never felt like that before. The routine allows me to focus and gets rid of any distractions or doubts I may have about my ability.' Kerri has very clear Reflect and Reset phases on the court. This helps her transition into the next point.

Kerri continues. 'Because it is a team sport you also have to help your partner recover from the previous point and get ready for the next point. Whenever we won a point we would celebrate that win by slapping hands. We would always communicate between points. It may have been as little as eye contact, a touch of the hand. This was especially important if it was your partner that made an error on the previous point. You have to let them know that it is okay that they made that mistake.'

Kerri even talked about the transition into arriving at the competition. For her, this transition is about getting rid of distractions. She prefers to listen to music rather than talk to people. 'I especially avoid talking to my competition, but I do like to hang out with my partner to develop that connection before I go out on the court. I think about the tactics we're going to use, I keep a record of plays and I look at my notes about what happened last time we played them.'

Micro-transitions are clearly important to Kerri and vital to better performance. Specifically, she has a clear process in her Reset phase where she focuses her mind so that she is not attached to an outcome. Let's slip into the Reset phase so you can 'show up' at your best in all parts of your life.

SUMMARY

- It is rare that single events fundamentally change who we are, our values and our behaviour.
- If you want to improve and exhibit new behaviours you must consciously choose to 'show up' and behave in that new way as you transition into each new space.
- The key to better performance is not to be attached to the outcome of the Second Space or worry about your performance.
- In the Second Space we can be driven by:
      –ego boost
      –avoiding failure
      –mastery of the task.
- Focus on mastery and being highly engaged in each space is incredibly important for our well-being. This is particularly important at work.
- How we 'show up' affects the people around us. Our moods are contagious.
- To get in the right mindset for mastery and engagement we need the right process (this process is covered in the next two chapters).
- Use the Reset phase of the Third Space to engage in the mastery of the task at hand and let go of attachment to the outcome.

Chapter 9

What is my clear intention?

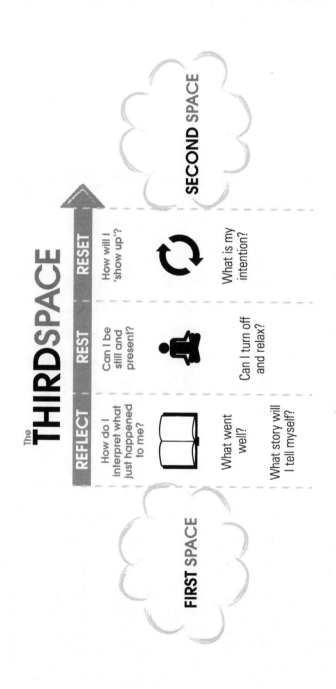

The first question you need to ask yourself in the Reset phase is: what is my intention in the next space? Having a clear intention for the next space is crucial to effective transitions. This means you have to spend a minute or two working out who you want to be when you enter that Second Space.

Do you ever get to work and have nothing to do? Do you get to work and think, 'If only someone would just give me more responsibility,' or 'I really need a few more projects to work on'? Probably not. Very few people fit into that category.

If you are a stay-at-home parent, you're not sleeping in and then bumming around the house looking for things to do. I look after my daughter by myself one day a week while my wife goes to work. It is by far the most exhausting and frantic day I have. By the time my wife comes home I'm ready for a glass of wine and a lie-down. Watching Chris go from full-time work to being a fulltime mother who works part-time, I've seen her workload more than double.

My father recently retired. When I asked him how it was going, he told me, 'Gee Ads, I don't know how I ever fitted in work. I am just flat out!'

We are all busy. What's the solution to this busyness? I have spoken to a number of stress management experts and work-life balance speakers. Their solution to the problem is to slow down, to simply do less. How practical is that message? Do you think you could go to work tomorrow and say to your boss, 'I read this great book last night and I have a new strategy – I am going to do less.' How do you think that message will go down at work? Not well. You simply can't say to your ten-month-old child, 'Mummy is going to back off a bit as I need some alone time and an opportunity to rest more. What this means for you is that you will have to step up and take on more responsibility.' We can't just 'slow down'. The key to handling this fast-paced world is having very clear intentions about what we are trying to achieve in each space we move into.

Having a clear intention is more important than ever when we are under stress. Harvard Professor Daniel Wegner has been obsessed with trying to understand 'thought suppression'. Why is it that when someone says, 'don't think of a pink elephant', that is all we can see? His research shows that it takes a lot of mental energy to suppress thoughts. While this works fine when we are calm, when we are stressed, our resources are low and we tend to behave in the exact way that we're trying to avoid.

'Don't tell them that they have put on a lot of weight since you last saw them.'

'Don't stuff up this presentation. Don't go blank and forget what you were going to say.'

'Don't mess up this shot. You'll be a laughing stock if you lose from here.'

The more we focus on what we don't want, the more likely it is to happen. Focusing on what we do want ensures a greater chance of success.[1]

CLARITY

To develop my intellectual property, I do research with universities, my company conducts surveys within organisations, and I draw on other people's research from across the globe. But by far the best information I source about workplaces comes from conversations at conference dinners. I attend many of these dinners each year and after a couple of drinks the information starts to fly. The most common thing I hear from honest employees is that they don't clearly understand what's expected of them at work. They say, 'Yeah, I have a job description and I have projects to work on, but I am not sure what I need to do. I lack clear goals. But it doesn't matter because my managers are so disorganised and frantic that they never keep me accountable to anything anyway.'

We lack clarity of intention – we don't know exactly what it is we're trying to achieve.

Marc K. Peter, Director of Technology and Business Development at LexisNexis Pacific, was quoted as saying that the 'average Australian employee only works 2.5 days per week'.[2] What are they doing with the other 2.5 days? They are usually trawling through information that does not have direct relevance to their day-to-day priorities. So let's examine this for a moment. Most people complain about how 'busy' they are at work yet the average person wastes 2.5 days per week on things that are not important. Hmm. Why are these workers wasting so much time? They're not clear on what exactly they are trying to achieve.

CLARITY OF VALUES

I visit at least 100 organisations a year and usually meet with senior staff. I ask all of them the same question: what are the values of this organisation? Eight times out of ten I am met with a blank stare. I recently met with the CEO of an organisation who, when confronted with that question, replied, 'Umm, there's a brochure in the foyer with them in it. Grab one on your way out.' 'Don't you know them?' I asked. He replied, 'Oh I used to. I think integrity is in there and maybe team work.' I grabbed the brochure. Neither of them were values. What I've found is that it's not that they don't care. It's usually that there are too many values, or they are worded in a way that is hard to remember or articulate. One organisation I worked with had 11 values. With that many, none of the staff could recite them all. If values are not front-of-mind, you might as well not have them. For values to have an impact on an organisation they must be memorable and they must be written in a language that we would use in day-to-day interactions.

In the mid-2000s, telecommunications company Vodafone had the following values:

Red

Rock solid
Restless

Red – this represented passion. It was an organisation that prided itself on being passionate and energetic.

Rock solid – they were dependable and knew their stuff.

Restless – the staff are always trying to improve, innovate and stay ahead of the competition.

To support this they constantly used these three terms in their language and had posters put up around the workplace.

Red – a guy with red face paint screaming at a football game.

Rock solid – an image of Uluru.

Restless – a rock climber climbing a sheer cliff face.

Everyone in the organisation had a very clear idea of how they had to behave.

The problem with the brain is that when there is no clarity to a task, it gets easily confused and overwhelmed, leading to poor performance and behaviour. I asked Ralph Norris, who was the CEO of Commonwealth Bank at the time, what he thought the biggest problem in business was. His reply: 'We make business too complicated. We try and focus on too many things and we're not razor sharp with our strategy. The result is a lot of activity that takes you nowhere. I run this bank on five simple principles. Unless you are very clear about exactly what you are trying to achieve, you will find it hard to get anything done.'

This lack of clarity in our work means we end up getting nothing done. But it's not just about work. We need clarity in all parts of our life.

During a workshop with a banking group, I talked to the team about the importance of clarity for business performance. Then I asked them what their clear intention was for the next month in the following five areas: as a leader, a parent, a partner, a friend and a person.

No one had a clear idea of what they wanted to achieve in each area. While each of them set strategies for their teams, they never thought about setting clear intention for the other parts of their lives. I worked with this group each month for the next six months. At each monthly check-in, we not only talked about business objectives, we also discussed objectives in each of these life areas. By the end of the six months there were significant improvements in each of these areas. The bankers became better leaders, partners, parents, friends and people. They simply worked out a clear intention for each part of their life.

I asked one man in the group what his intention was as a husband for the next month. Very seriously, he said, 'My wife and I don't talk to each other anymore. After we put the kids to bed, we eat dinner in front of the TV and do our own thing. It's not good. My intention is to talk to and get to know my wife again.' He went home that night, walked through the front door and announced to his wife, 'Tonight we're going to have dinner.'

'That's great, genius,' she said. 'We have dinner every night.'

'No,' he told her. 'Tonight will be different. We're going to sit at the dinner table, no TV, no kids and we are going to talk.' His wife just looked at him.

'What have you done?'

Apparently, it took him two hours to convince her that he was not having an affair. They started to have dinner together each night at the table. He said the first week was brutal as they experienced extreme TV withdrawal. But after a week they looked forward to it. He said he learned things about his wife that he never knew.

At the start of every week I ask myself what my clear intention is in the following areas: as a business owner, a presenter, a husband, a father, a friend and a person.

Each time I move through the Third Space into one of these roles I ensure that I have this intention at the front of my mind. At the end of each week, I rate myself on how well I have gone. Not only does this technique help get things done but it also dramatically reduces my stress levels as I feel more in control of my life. In addition, it gives me a sense of achievement and shows me that I am progressing. This last one is vital for happiness because one of the drivers of happiness is having a sense of achievement and reflecting on the fact that we are moving forward.

The first step in the Reset phase is to clearly articulate your intention for the next space.

CLARITY IN SURGERY

When you think about micro-transitions and having to jump between multiple roles that are very demanding, the job of a heart surgeon is certainly one that comes to mind. Cardiac surgeons have a very difficult job. They jump between surgery, consultations with patients, admin, doing research, teaching, keeping a home life and staying up-to-date with the latest research findings and techniques. If they are on call, they might be at a family function and suddenly have to rush into hospital to operate on someone. Surgeons take transitioning to another level.

In my search to understand how they cope with the multiple and extremely different transitions they make, I interviewed Dr Ravinay Bhindi MBBS PhD FRACP FESC, Senior Lecturer at the University of Sydney Department of Cardiology, located at Royal North Shore Hospital. Dr Bhindi makes a great case study because in addition to being a surgeon, he conducts research and is also married with young children.

I was fortunate enough to steal 30 minutes of his precious time and outlined the concept of the Third Space and micro-transitions to him. I asked him how he was able to transition so effectively. Dr Bhindi was incredibly clear on his intention. He said: 'My intention is to give every one of my patients the best possible care and experience they can have when they are in my care. Every time I deal with a patient I say to myself as I walk in, "If this was my mother, father, brother, wife or child, how would I want them to be treated?" I remind myself that each person's case is incredibly important to them.

'You can go from treating someone with terminal cancer to talking to someone about their elevated cholesterol levels. While cholesterol may seem trivial compared to cancer, for that person with high cholesterol it is equally important. I have to invest as much energy, care and focus to the small cases as I do to the big cases.'

His intention allows him to be completely present and absorbed in each space he moves into. Dr Bhindi then went on to say that being present and caring allows him to not worry about the previous space or the next space. Being present allows him to transition effectively. Interestingly, he said that the emergency situations are the easiest to transition into because his adrenaline is pumping and his focus needs to be high.

The hardest transition for Dr Bhindi was going back home after having to break bad news to the family of a patient being treated. 'It's hard not to carry the baggage home with you when things don't go according to plan and you get a bad result for someone. But I think about my intention for the family and it helps me be focused and present in the home space.'

Dr Bhindi's intention at work is to treat each person with empathy, respect and care. Many other doctors have told me that in medical school they were encouraged to not care too deeply about their patients, that they would never survive as a doctor if they did. I floated this idea by Dr Bhindi and his response was that the benefits of caring far outweighed its downsides. He believes that his desire to care actually allows him to move onto the next space. If you truly care about the next patient you become present with them and therefore not as much baggage comes with you. He was not delusional, though. 'Yes, sometimes if you care about a patient who has a bad result, you can take that home with you and let it affect your home life.' But overall, he believed that caring for your patients made you a far better doctor.

Following my interview with Dr Bhindi, I was invited to talk to a group of GPs about how they could work better with their patients to help them introduce healthy habits into their lifestyle. Because GPs are so busy I gave them a very simple three-step change model. During lunch with the group afterwards, a couple of them told me, 'I don't bother talking to my patients about lifestyle change anymore. I tried it and they don't change, so I can't be bothered anymore.'

How does their intention differ to Dr Bhindi's? Dr Bhindi's intention is focused on the care of the patient and getting the best outcome for them, while these specific GPs were focused on themselves and the fact that it annoyed them to keep having that conversation. Their focus was to take the easy option, to not help their patients change. Which intention do you think will create the best experience for the patient?

CLEAR INTENTION IS SAVING HEALTHCARE

While doing my research for the presentation to the doctors, I came across an amazing case study profiled in the *Wall Street Journal* and the *Economist* of a surgeon who is changing the way surgery is performed.

Heart disease is the biggest killer in the western world. The average heart surgery in the US costs between $20,000 and $100,000. In Australia, Medibank Private has reported that some open heart surgeries can be as much as $180,000.[3] A recent boom in heart disease and obesity has meant the cost to our medical system is exploding. One doctor is turning this around single-handedly. Dr Devi Shetty performs open heart surgery for $2000 in Bangalore, southern India. He is making surgery affordable by changing the way in which people are operated on. Dr Shetty looked outside his industry to the car industry; he learned from them, and then implemented their systems into the surgical process. He has introduced Toyota-like production line systems to operate on people's hearts.

In the western world, heart surgery is primarily conducted by one person: the surgeon. What Dr

Shetty has done is build a large team of surgeons and give each member of the team a specific job. Surgeon A makes the incision and 'cracks' the chest, Surgeon B then opens the artery, Surgeon C inserts the stent, and so forth. The operating theatres resemble a production line, with multiple surgeries happening all at once.

The hospital in Bangalore has around 1000 beds (the average American cardiac hospital has approximately 160 beds) and churns through around 600 operations in a week.[4] How does this work? If you only have one job you become very, very good at that job. The production line also speeds up the process, which means less time under anaesthetic for the patient and an increased volume of operations occurring. Everyone wins.

A western surgeon will, over their lifetime, perform on average 2400 to 3000 surgeries. In Dr Shetty's hospital, surgeons are completing more than that by the time they are in their early thirties.

Dr Shetty is reported to have performed more than 15,000 heart operations, and other members of his team more than 10,000. When this story broke, surgeons across the world said that the quality would drop because of the large volume of operations. The average mortality rate after surgery in the US is 1.9 per cent. For Dr Shetty's team, it is 1.4 per cent (2008).[5] Their surgery outcomes are better!

This is totally revolutionising the healthcare of Dr Shetty's country. The poorest are now able to afford heart surgery. This is amazing considering the health system is often criticised for being resistant to change.

Would this system work in Australia or the US? Maybe. The critical block will be whether the Western surgeons have an intention to protect their status and pay packet or an intention to provide a better outcome for patients. In a country with rising healthcare costs, we need innovations like this to change the playing field and make healthcare affordable for all.

What I love about Dr Shetty is that his intention is to provide better patient care and to save the health system by making care affordable to the poor and needy.

CONNECTING INTENTION TO PURPOSE

As shown in the above examples, carrying a clear intention into the Second Space allows you to 'show up' and perform better. We can make our intention even more powerful by linking it to a compelling and moving purpose.

I was asked to do a workshop with administration staff from various schools. One of the challenges the schools faced was a lack of engagement at work from this group. Many of them saw their job as not that important, and when they interacted with parents or students they were not as warm or helpful as they could be. During the session, I asked them to write down their job description. Over the next three minutes I noticed that their lists looked something like this:

- answer phone
- file
- send emails
- draft letters
- take enquiries from students
- manage principal's diary

I then told the administration workers the following story, which I heard during a conference presentation by Barry Schwartz, a US-based psychologist and professor at Swarthmore College:

A group of hospital cleaners were gathered together for a research study, and grouped into great cleaners (well respected, admired by the other staff in the hospital, positive feedback from patients) and poor cleaners (not known to the other staff, low level of positive feedback). The cleaners in the poor-performing group were asked if their job was hard, to which they replied, 'No, it's easy. Anyone could do it.' They were then asked to outline their job description. It included the following – empty bins, clean floors, vacuum, dispose of sharps and so on – not a job most of us would consider difficult. But when the first group was asked whether their job was hard, they said, 'Yes. It's incredibly difficult and takes years to master.' The researchers were surprised by this and asked what their job description was. They responded, 'Our job is to improve the experience the people have when they come into the hospital.' One said, 'For example, I was told by my supervisor to vacuum the waiting room, when I noticed that there was a family sleeping in the corner. I asked the nursing staff who they were. It turned out they had been there for two days and this was the first time they had had any sleep so I left the vacuuming to the end of my shift.'

And another said, 'There was a young boy who was in a coma; his dad was holding a bedside vigil. I cleaned the boy's room while the dad was out. When he came back he found me in the room next door and started yelling at me, saying that I had skipped his son's room because he was in a coma and claiming that I didn't think his son deserved a clean room. I started to argue back when I realised that he just needed to blow off some steam. So I let him! After he finished, I apologised and redid his son's room. It was more important for him to release some frustration than for me to argue the point.' What an amazing intention to have as they transition into work. Their intention was to improve the experience the patients had during their stay.

After telling them this story I then encouraged the admin staff to reflect again on their job description and write that down. This time they came up with the following:

- I am the face of the school.
- I create the first impression of the school.
- I help the students who are in crisis.

- I help calm down the parents who are angry about a school-related issue.
- I am a sounding board for the principal.
- I keep the school running smoothly.
- I help make people's day.
- I am a counsellor to the teachers.
- The students confide in me the things they can't tell their teachers.
- I facilitate education.

Once they articulated these their physiology changed, they sat up straighter and became more enthusiastic. Finding their intention and meaning led the staff to 'show up' with a totally different mindset.

ST JUDE HOSPITAL – BRENE BROWN

I attended a weekend retreat with Brene Brown, a research professor at the University of Houston Graduate College of Social Work. During this workshop she told the story of how she went to visit St Jude Children's Research Hospital. To give you some background, St Jude is one of the best paediatric cancer hospitals on the planet. It is internationally recognised as completely changing how we treat children with cancer. In fact, the medical breakthroughs from this hospital alone have taken cancer survival rates from below 20 per cent to over 80 per cent. Staggering, when you think about it.

Brene went to visit the hospital and got into a lift with a woman.

'What do you do here?' Brene asked her.

The woman answered, 'I cure cancer.'

'Really?' Brene replied. 'So you're a researcher?'

'No I'm the cook.'

Confused, Brene then asked, 'Sorry, if you're the cook, how do you cure cancer?'

'I feed the researchers. If they don't eat, they can't work. So I cure cancer.'

Brene then met the head of marketing. When Brene asked what was it he did at the hospital, she got the same reply:

'I cure cancer.'

Everyone she met said that they did the same thing: 'I cure cancer.'

Now, that is a clear purpose and intention.

Unsurprisingly, for the last six years, St Jude Children's Research Hospital has been named as one of the top institutions to work for in the annual 'Best Places to Work in Academia' list by *Scientist* magazine.

With such a clear intention that is tied to a compelling purpose, do you think that workplace would have a buzz to it? Do you think people would be driven to achieve? I think so.

The only reason the St Jude hospital exists is because someone followed through on their intention. Danny Thomas was a struggling entertainer who was desperate to make it in the business. One day he prayed to St Jude Thaddeus, the patron saint of lost causes. He pledged: if you make me famous I will build you a shrine that will change the world. Years later St Jude did his part and Danny became an internationally known entertainer. Danny followed through on his side of the deal and in 1962 the hospital was opened.

MAKING A DIFFERENCE

When you think of life insurance what comes to mind? Life insurance does not tend to give you a warm fuzzy feeling in your stomach. Life insurance gets a bad rap. In part, this is not undeserved. The only time my life insurance company contacts me is to tell me that my premiums have gone up. It's not a letter I look forward to as they tell me that (a) I am now older and (b) I owe them more money. Not exactly a line from the book *How to win Friends and Influence People.* Bearing this in mind, I thought my meeting with the new executive general manager of Asteron Life would be an interesting one.

As I sat in the foyer, a very large and enthusiastic man bounded towards me with an outstretched hand.

'Hey Adam, I'm Jordan Hawke. Great to meet you.' Jordan had just taken over running Asteron Life and was planning his first conference to set the scene for this plans and leadership. When we sat down he said to me, 'I believe that the relationship between an insurance company and the client is a dysfunctional one.' Now that's not something you'd expect a life insurance general manager to admit. 'It's a terrible experience. There is no relationship with the customer, and the whole industry is about guilting people into taking out insurance. The client doesn't want to do it and the insurance company doesn't improve their life. Nothing is positive about the relationship at all and we at Asteron Life are going to change the way life insurance is conducted in this country.

'We're going to make taking out insurance a superb experience for the customer and the adviser. This will go a long way to solving the underinsurance issue in Australia.'

Normally I would be sceptical of this message but it was impossible not to like him and get caught up in his vision. You could tell that this guy genuinely gave a damn and had a clear intention.

'For any organistion to be great you have to pin something to your mast,' he said. 'What we will pin to our mast is, we are going to be a life/risk specialist aligned with independent financial planners, with insurance at our core and care at our heart.'

Before I presented to the Asteron Life conference, Jordan stood up and gave his first address to the entire company. He was outstanding. He talked about his vision to make insurance a positive experience and that their purpose at Asteron Life was to pay claims and make a difference to people's lives in a time of need. What kind of insurance company sees their job as paying claims? Don't insurance companies focus on not paying claims? But Jordan continued to talk about purpose, meaning and intention. You could tell that people in the group were moved, but there was an air of scepticism.

Over the next four years I was regularly engaged by Jordan to work with his team on many of the principles covered in this book. We talked about the Third Space, and about showing up, celebrating victory as a team, about our explanation style, about having purpose, having behaviour aligned to intention, regulating our thoughts and emotions, and being present. They were a dream client: they took all these strategies on board and executed them. In addition, Asteron Life as a business really stepped up. It seriously examined its direction and what it wanted to be known for. They mapped out a clear strategy and executed it. One of the senior executives made a comment to me: 'Before Jordan came on board we had a great culture. We still have a great culture but now we have direction. We used to be nice people and now we're nice people with an edge. We now have a direction and a plan.'

KEY ACTIONS THAT GOT TRACTION

Watching this whole process unfold I noticed two important things Jordan did as a leader. The first was connecting each person to purpose. How did he do this? He told stories. Whenever Asteron Life paid a claim, he got the organisation together and told the story of how they had just helped someone in need. He told stories of families who had lost a family member and now they can keep their house and pay for the funeral because of the money Asteron Life had given them. Then he showed each person in the organisation how their actions contributed to that outcome, from the people who answered the phones to the sales team and the underwriters.

It took time and it took a truckload of work. Jordan and his leadership team had to be relentless and unwavering in their actions. Some things worked and some did not. However, the employees at Asteron Life started to realise that they were making a massive difference to people's lives. They realised their jobs were really important (having lost a friend to a heart attack at the age of 39, a friend who had a young family with no insurance, I can see this importance). Because they had a purpose and, more importantly, were shown that what they did on a daily basis contributed to that purpose, people started to 'show up' to work differently. They were more engaged, more energetic and more focused. They stopped showing up to do a job and instead focused on making a difference. The word got out about what a unique place Asteron Life was to work at and people from other insurance companies began to knock on their door. They became an employer of choice and their turnover was incredibly low. This clear intention allowed their culture to blossom.

The second thing Jordan did was to model the behaviour that he expected from his team. He came to work with energy, he treated people with respect, he was approachable and each day he exhibited the passion that he talked about. One employee told me that during busy periods Jordan was not beyond wheeling around a cart with dinner on it to feed the people who were working late.

The big question is: did this make a commercial difference?

Through their high-performance culture, Asteron Life became a workplace that fostered and bred innovation. Usually when you take out insurance you are required to complete a Personal Medical Attendant Report (PMAR). This is when the insurance company collects your entire medical history. It's an incredibly arduous process for everyone involved. Asteron Life was the first company to ask the question: do PMARs actually alter how much a person has to pay for insurance? What Asteron Life found was that it did not make any difference to their decision, yet it cost a lot of money to do it and it was a pain for everyone involved. So Asteron Life stopped asking for mandatory PMARs.

In addition, they introduced an initiative called 'First Response Unit'. What this means is that if you put in a claim for a condition (illness or injury), the insurance company will generally know how long you will be off work for. So Asteron Life now pays you that amount of money upfront. If it takes six months to recover, you get paid upfront six months' worth of income. The great thing is that if you go back after three months you keep the difference. However, if you don't go back after six months they will assess the claim again. What they find is that when the immediate financial pressure is taken off, people recover faster.

From 2003 to 2008 Asteron Life did not grow (in terms of writing new business) faster than two per cent per year. When Jordan joined, he achieved the following revenue growth for the company:

- 2009–28%
- 2010–13%
- 2011–15%

When I interviewed Jordan he told me that in the previous 12 months the life/risk market grew at 5.85 per cent. Asteron Life's share grew by 28.55 per cent and the overall value of the business increased. It just goes to show what you can achieve when you are clear on your intention and you execute it.

CLEAR INTENTIONS FACILITATE CREATIVITY

During my interview with the Impossible Institute's CEO Dan Gregory, he pointed out that the clearer and tighter the brief (another word for intention) in advertising, the greater your opportunity to be creative. Most people think that tight parameters stifle creativity as they think we need room to move and have complete freedom. But this is actually worse as you just have more opportunities to be wrong. In contrast, if you have a really strong anchor point you can pull on that in any direction. The creative prayer in advertising is, 'Lord, grant me the freedom of a tight brief.' Dan gave the example of the company Pirelli Tyres. Their brief to the advertising company was: it doesn't matter how powerful your car is, if the tyre does not hold you on the road that power is pointless. This is a super tight brief and because it is so tight you can express it in a million different ways. In response to this the advertising agency came up with an advert which had Olympic sprinter Carl Lewis in the starting blocks wearing bright red high heels, accompanied by the line 'Power is nothing without Control'. They came up with a whole host of ads that won awards. One of the most popular television advertisements showed Carl Lewis running along the New York skyline, up the Statue of Liberty, jumping on the Chrysler building and so on – all in bare feet. At the end of the ad he stops and lifts one foot up to reveal the tread of a Pirelli tyre blended into the sole of his foot.

A loose brief is analogous to someone walking up to you and saying, 'Make up an original joke to make me laugh.' That is much harder to do than if someone walks up to you and says, 'Make up an original joke about men being bad at fore-play.' The greater the level of clarity, the easier creativity flows.

TRANSITIONING INTO A TOUGH JOB

I was on a flight to Asia and the movie they were showing was *Up in the Air,* starring George Clooney. In this movie George's character Ryan Bingham flies around the US firing people. It's his job. Watching this movie I was thinking, wow. That has to be a tough thing to transition in and out of. To do this job effectively you would have to be pretty heartless, as is Ryan's case. There is a scene in the movie where Ryan explains to a colleague that that moment when a person can look into another person's eyes and feel a connection of souls is not something he experiences. He's a character quite devoid of emotions, which is how he is able to do what he does for a living.

The question is whether it's possible to transition in and out of this role and not be cold-hearted.

Murry Taylor has had a very successful career as a manager in various organisations. His specialisation is revenue protection and risk and his job is to prevent theft, both internal and external. He is exceptional at what he does. In his last role, in less than 12 months he reduced his company's loss by such an extent it led to a bottom line improvement of $6.1 million. In addition, the efficiencies he introduced to the company saved $644,000 on security spending. That is a return any CEO would be happy with.

During this time he and his team terminated just under 200 staff members for theft and fraud (some of whom were senior executives), with, it's worth noting, zero unfair dismissals. One would think that such an individual would be cold-hearted, almost cyborg-like, with a vendetta against the world. Murry is the opposite. He's warm, funny and incredibly passionate about leadership and investing in the relationships he has at work. During his 18 months in this role, the staff turnover in his team was zero per cent (compared to 70–75 per cent across the company). You need to be a great leader to keep your staff engaged when their role is as stressful as investigating and sacking people.

When I met Murry, I simply asked, 'How? How do you transition in and out of terminating so many people? How do you terminate someone knowing they have to go home and tell their family and then go back to your desk and keep working. Or go home and be present with your own family?'

He answered, 'My role had so many facets. One moment I'm putting together a presentation for the board, and the next I'm terminating someone more senior to me and escorting them off the premises. Then I go back and have a meeting with my team where I need to be there for them and support them and give them strategic guidance. How I transition in and out of this role is due to three key things.

'Firstly, I focus on the purpose of what I am doing. I only terminate people if they have been caught for theft or fraud. I focus on the fact that this business is supporting my livelihood and the livelihood of thousands of others and this person who is stealing is threatening all our livelihoods. Keeping that intention front of mind helps me greatly.

'Secondly, I'm incredibly organised and I have a clear process and system that I follow. I never go in there cold. I know exactly what I need to do and the evidence I have is incredibly clear.

'Finally, I focus on staying calm. Some of the people I terminate get very angry and upset. Some even threaten me physically. I just stay calm and bring it back to the facts. I focus on the process. I don't judge them or attack their character. I keep control over my emotions, which actually helps them to calm down as well. In particular, I make sure to enter the room feeling very calm myself.'

Murray concluded by saying, 'As I am walking into a termination I remind myself of these three things.'

A clear intention allows Murray to 'show up' in the best possible way by transitioning in and out of a task that would scare the hell out of the average person.

WHAT ARE YOU SELLING?

No matter who, we are all selling something all the time. Whether we're trying to get our child to sleep, score a first date with someone we're interested in or receive the nod in a job interview. Selling is simply the ability to convince other people to agree with your point of view. Chris Helder is one of Australia's leading experts in sales. He has a long career as a successful salesperson and sales coach. I spoke to him about the Third Space and its application to sales. He was immediately excited about the concept on a number of levels. Firstly, he said that too many salespeople are desperate to get the sale and because of that they bring the baggage of where they have been with them and ultimately it affects their performance. It is vital that they clear their last appointment away (the Reflect phase as discussed in chapters 5 and 6) so they can focus on the next appointment. This is particularly important if you had a terrible result in the previous sales situation. You must break that energy. You need to learn from it – what went right, what went wrong – and then change your mindset to leave it behind.

He continued: 'Secondly, where this transitional space is really important is in the Reset phase. The times when I got smashed in a sales situation were when I was unprepared and unclear on my intention. The average salesperson is so busy selling that they don't take the time to understand what is going on for that client. What are their challenges? Do I know anything personal about them – their kids, their hobbies, or where they are trying to go with the business?' I was on the phone to Chris while he was driving to meet a coaching client. 'After I hang up from you I will remind myself about my client's family situation, what he likes to do in his spare time, what we talked about last time to do with his business. It's important that I consciously take five minutes to focus on him and become present with that moment.'

As a salesperson you need to be absolutely clear about your intention for that meeting; what you're trying to achieve. It may be that for your next sales meeting your clear intention is to understand your client's current challenges. You're not 'showing up' to sell at all. The intention in this next meeting is simply to understand their world a little more.

Another technique that Chris uses is determining the story he will tell. When you are selling you need to be clear about the story that you are going to tell. Stories resonate with people and engage them on an emotional level. The story must have four parts:

Part 1 – Tell a story of another client who has a similar challenge to the person you're meeting with.

Part 2 – Outline what the other client discovered about their challenge and how they overcame it.

Part 3 – Point out that the client in front of you is in a similar situation.

Part 4 – Then point out what a shame it would be to not take advantage of that opportunity.

Trying to wing this story is impossible. Preparation and clear intention is key.

Chris does the following in his Reset phase:

- Physical preparation: high energy, good posture, eye contact.
- Self-talk: what is the story I bring to this moment?
- Mental preparation: am I focused and being present in that moment? Am I clear about my intention and what I want to achieve?

The Reset phase is all about clarity of intention, not worrying about our performance and being detached from the outcome. As you travel through the Third Space you may not always have time to Reflect or Rest but you must always Reset.

Examples of clear intentions:

Situation	Intention
Transitioning home	To be a patient and caring parent who does not yell at his or her children and is empathetic to his or her partner's day.
Transitioning into an internal meeting	To create an open and safe environment so people are not afraid to share ideas.
Transitioning into a sales meeting	To listen and understand their business challenges.
A coaching session with a direct report	To understand what the report is enjoying in his or her role and what s/he would like to do more of to increase his or her level of engagement.
A presentation	'The three key points that I want them to walk out of the room with are...'
With your children	To be playful, present, calm and accepting.
Spending time with friends	To be fun, non-judgemental, supportive and relaxed.

Situation	Intention
Writing an article	To be provocative and challenge people.

SUMMARY

- We are all busy so we have to be more discerning about tasks we will focus on.
- Having clarity around your intention for each space is critical.
- If you can connect your intention to a driving purpose, even better.
- Clear intention allows you to be creative and keeps you focused in the face of tough circumstance.
- Sales make the world go around. We're all selling something. Working out your intention allows you to communicate well and maximises the chance of you getting the desired result.

Chapter 10

It's not me, it's you

In the previous chapter we learned that intention is vitally important to how we 'show up' right. However, intention on its own is not enough. We must ensure that our actions and behaviours are congruent with that intention. You have to walk your talk. This is the final phase in Reset, where you ask yourself what behaviour you want to exhibit. It won't do any good to walk through your front door, tell your family you're relaxed and have left work behind you, and then bite their heads off.

WE ARE ALL NUTS

'If you're pretty crazy then you're in good company because the human race as a whole is out of its goddamn head. Now all of you, of course, know this about others – about your mother and father and sisters and brothers and friends and wives and husbands. You know how nutty they are. Now the problem is to admit this about yourself, and then do something about it.'

This confronting, hilarious and at the same time hard-hitting statement was made by Albert Ellis, one of the most well-respected clinical psychologists to draw breath and a pioneer of Cognitive Behaviour

Therapy. While reading this for the first time it dawned on me that he is actually right!

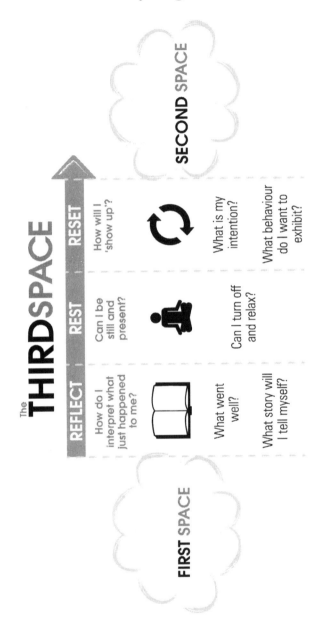

Whenever I finish a presentation on management dysfunction, the most common thing I hear from people is, 'Oh, if only my partner was here. They need this stuff. They're driving me crazy!' Or, 'If only my team was here. They're all dysfunctional. I mean, I'm fine, but they need to hear this stuff.' No one has ever come up to me and said, 'Wow, I just realised that *I'm* the unreasonable, illogical, dysfunctional pain in the butt in my team. I have been stirring up trouble and undermining my manager for years, I really need to improve my behaviour at work.' They talk about how if only everyone else would get it together, then they'd be okay.

I believe one of the biggest problems in society today is that people 'show up' thinking, 'It's not ME, it's YOU!'

We seem to chronically lack self-awareness of our behaviour. Being self-aware is an immense skill that is needed by all of us whether we are a friend, parent, partner, leader or a team member. One of the big mistakes we make is that we focus all our attention on the 'doing' that we forget about the 'being' part. During our day we have to look at how we are being, not just what we are doing.

When I first began working with leaders around improving their performance, I observed that the normal process for a leader in an organisation who was not performing well was for the organisation to hire a coach to help that leader improve his or her performance.

The problem was that the only people in the conversation were the leader and the coach. No one else. The coach would ask questions such as, 'How do you think that impacts on the team?' 'How could you look at this differently?' I asked one coach why they didn't involve the team in the process. Their response was very philosophical. 'The leader has all the answers inside them. I'm just there to help pull the answers out.' The problem with this process is that it hangs its hat on the fact that the leader has all the answers. Well guess what? Leaders don't have all the answers. They lack self-awareness about their own ability to 'show up' and how they affect the people around them.

When I spoke to leaders I would often ask questions such as: 'What is your empathy like?'

They would usually reply, 'Oh, I am very empathetic. I know what it's like to walk in their shoes. I feel that I am in touch with my team and I understand them.'

'Do you create a good culture?'

'Definitely. I create an environment where people can express themselves to me without retribution. I see myself as a coach who fosters my team's development and I have a strong relationship with each and every one of them.'

I would then speak to the team to get feedback on their leadership style. I heard things like: '(My boss is) an egomaniac whose only focus is to better their career; he is a tyrant who uses fear to get people to engage.' I was gobsmacked at how many leaders lacked self-awareness of their behaviour.

How they showed up did not relate to how they thought they showed up. In fact, in most cases they were nowhere near it.

CORPORATE SOCIOPATH

I was asked by a law firm to meet with one of their partners about coaching him around his behaviour in the firm. It sounded quite straightforward. I then asked why they thought he needed coaching.

'Well, he has gone through 18 junior lawyers in the last six years, and the last one that worked with him almost had a nervous breakdown.' That's when the alarm bells went off. This was going to be a bigger challenge than I thought.

In preparation for my meeting, I interviewed a number of the people in the firm and they painted a unanimous and unfavourable picture of him. They all told me that while he was the best technical lawyer they had ever seen, he was also the most controlling, impersonal, manipulative and critical person they had ever worked with. The interesting thing is that he was never aggressive or overtly angry; they said he was very passive, but would subtly tear away at their self-worth and confidence. Employees were afraid to send printing to the communal printer because he would pick up their printing (which had nothing to do with him) and approach them to point out what was wrong with their work and how they should fix it.

I greeted him in his office's meeting room. We had a very brief conversation about his background and what led him to the firm. He seemed pleasant enough.

We sat down and I cut to the chase.

'We both know why we're here. It's to discuss the high turnover of staff you have had in your area. I would like to get your take on the situation.'

I had a list of names in front of me and I asked him to run me through what happened that led to each of these people leaving his division. He proceeded to go through the list of people and tell me what was wrong with 'them'.

'Well, she was an absolute nut case. I think she actually had mental health issues. The second one was incredibly incompetent and the third one, well, he had no work ethic.'

On and on he went telling me what was wrong with all these people. I was stunned.

At the end of the list I asked him, 'What was it about your behaviour that contributed to them leaving?' I have never seen someone look at me with such contempt and disgust.

'I don't understand. I just told you the problem,' he said. 'They were incompetent. If these lawyers were any good they would stay. What have I got to do with it?'

I kept pressing. 'If they're all so hopeless, why have some of them gone off to flourish in other parts of the firm?'

To which he replied, 'They aren't going well. The other partners in the firm just say that to keep them happy and to make me look bad. None of these people is a lawyer's bootlace.'

Getting him to admit that his behaviour may have contributed to the situation was like trying to raise the *Titanic* with a dinghy. In desperation, I asked him if he wanted to work on his behaviour with a series of coaching sessions. He agreed. I told him that the first step was for him to identify a series of key stake-holders in the business to give him feedback on his behaviour. Specifically, what he does well and what he needs to improve on.

'No.'

'No what?' I asked.

'No. I refuse to let anyone give me feedback on my behaviour.'

'But you'll get to choose who gives you feedback,' I said.

'I don't care,' was his reply.

'Well how do you expect to be a better leader if you don't ask any of the people you lead about how you can do it better?'

The next line was my favourite. 'I'm self-aware enough to know what I need to improve on and what I don't.' At this point, I wrapped up the interview and left. I told the HR manager I was not interested in working with someone who was unwilling to work with me. I later found out that they removed him out of the practice because the impact he had on the culture was not worth the money he made them.

With this realisation I completely changed the way I worked with leaders.

A NEW APPROACH

My work with leaders began to focus more and more on the team's assessment. I would ask the team three simple questions:

1. What should your leader keep doing?
2. What do they need to stop doing?
3. What should they start doing?

Then, armed with this information, I began to work with the leaders to help them to stop certain behaviours or introduce new ones.

The results were instant and effective. The other beautiful thing was that we involved the team in the change process. We would inform the team of the behaviours the leader was trying to work on and to be on the lookout for them. The team would also give me regular feedback on how the leader was progressing. All the leaders I have worked with who truly embraced this process saw great results. We also observed that this process resulted in huge shifts in culture and better team performance. Part of the positive shift in culture was due to the leader being transparent and open. However, the challenge was that this process required the leader to be very brave. Being this transparent and vulnerable requires guts. Some leaders I work with are terrified by this process and do not have the bravery to stick it out, but it shows that they are not serious about changing.

This process applies to all relationships such as with your partner, friends and family. Admitting that there are behaviours that you need to improve and work on, and including the other person in the process, greatly improves the quality of that relationship.

DOES YOUR BEHAVIOUR MATCH YOUR INTENTION?

While it's important to have a clear intention as we transition, we must ensure that our behaviour is aligned to that intention. This requires us to develop self-awareness about our behaviour, and understand the impact of that behaviour on each new space we move into.

I have had the pleasure of working with Steve Lundin, who is the author of the best-selling book, *Fish.* He is currently a Professor of Business at Griffith University. One of the courses he teaches is Responsible Leadership in the MBA program. The concept of asking leaders how they 'show up' really resonated with him.

'The number one thing leaders can do is have an accurate look at themselves and how they "show up" and affect the people at work and at home,' he said. 'Most leaders never allow others to give them honest feedback and never ask for it. They assume they know how they are "showing up" or simply do not care.'

We do this in our personal lives too. Often, we might think our friend/partner as being unreasonable yet we see our behaviour as being totally appropriate.

One of the greatest dysfunctions in any group of people (family, workplace, social group) is that its members have a low level of self-awareness and a high level of judgement and contempt for others. We often think that our behaviour is reasonable and are quick to judge the people who lead/manage us, our team members or the people we lead. Within corporations, we tend to judge other business units all too often. People in finance judge the marketing department. People in procurement judge the human resources department. Administration looks at IT and says 'Gee, if only IT could just get it together, we'd be productive!' We judge those other departments without a clear understanding of their challenges or pressures.

Why do we lack this self-awareness? Well, that's the $64,000 question. It comes down to a number of reasons:

- It is easier to blame others than look at our own behaviour.
- It feels good to judge others, because it simply feels good to be so right.
- When we publicly blame/judge/persecute others we elevate ourselves in the social hierarchy.
- It is a blow to our ego to admit we are wrong.
- We simply can't entertain the thought that we are not perfect.

- We don't realise we are wrong. (Author and speaker Kathryn Schulz has made famous the topic of being wrong. What she points out is that it doesn't feel like anything to be wrong, in fact it feels a lot like being right.)
- Our behaviour is often not aligned with our intention.

Let's explore the last one in detail.

You can have amazing intentions and, at the same time, have profoundly dysfunctional behaviour. I'm sure there are very few managers who get out of bed and say, 'Alright. Today I'm going to belittle my staff, make them feel worthless, give them no freedom and be massively controlling.' And yet many employees will tell you that this is exactly what their manager does. Even priests can be dysfunctional.

At Princeton University, a study was conducted called the Darley-Batson Good Samaritan Experiment, where they observed the behaviour of Divinity students (people studying to be priests). The researchers asked each of the students to write a sermon on The Good Samaritan (the Bible story about someone going out of their way to help others) and scheduled them in to deliver this sermon to a group. The day before their seminars, the researchers called each student into a room and announced, 'Sorry, we made a huge scheduling mistake. Your sermon actually started 10 minutes ago. You have to go there now!'

The student tore out of the meeting and headed for the lecture room. The researchers had hired an actor to fake a heart attack in front of them and observed to see if the student stopped to help. The results were surprising. Very few of them stopped to help the dying man. Why? Because they had to go and teach people how to care and help others in need. Was their intention good? Yes, profoundly good. Was their behaviour dysfunctional? Absolutely. It's so easy to get caught up in doing things, that our behaviour becomes misaligned to our intention.

I had firsthand experience of this a number of years ago. I asked the team I was leading to give me anonymous feedback on how I led and managed them. After receiving the feedback I didn't sleep for three nights. It was scathing. They thought that sure, I was a nice guy, but I drove them insane. They made a list detailing how I drove them insane, and it was so long! When I looked at the list, I realised that I did those things to motivate the team, to show them that I cared. While my intention had been very good, my behaviour was dysfunctional, and I was completely unaware of it.

GOOD PEOPLE CAN STILL BE DYSFUNCTIONAL

I often work with leadership teams who have just received 360-degree feedback (where your peers, as well as people from positions above and below you in the organisation, give feedback on your behaviour). They are always shocked at how their behaviour is perceived by others. In many cases, the leaders are given one-on-one debrief sessions in order to cope with the feedback they've just received.

I run a workshop called 'It's not me, it's you'. In one particular session, we talked as a group about how it's okay to admit that we get things wrong and that we are never going to act perfectly all the time. We talked about how, even if we sometimes exhibit dysfunctional behaviours, we can still be a good person. Following this, there was a collective sigh of relief. People opened up about feeling that receiving negative feedback on their behaviour was a personal attack on them. It started a conversation that we rarely have and yet we so desperately need. It opened up dialogue and made it okay to have these challenging conversations.

One woman in the group told us she had a great leader in her organisation. She said what made him great was that he asked for feedback on his behaviour and took it on board without taking offence. 'One day I told my manager that when things were very busy and we had tight deadlines, he became aggressive and curt. This was really unsettling for the team. I told him that it reduces our productivity and shoots up our stress levels. The great thing was his response to this feedback. He said he'd had no idea he acted like this, then apologised and said, "I really want to work on this. When we have our monthly catch-ups can you let me know how I'm going?"'

So how do we improve our self-awareness about how we 'show up'?

1. Make a concerted effort to objectively observe your behaviour. Is it reasonable? Do you get involved in office gossip? Are you overly sensitive? Do you persecute people in the organisation behind their back rather than talking to them face-to-face about issues? Practise real-time self-awareness.

2. Examine how your behaviour impacts on other people around you. How do they behave when you're around? Do your family members tense up when you come home? Does your mood bring down the whole team that you work with? Is your team reserved and cagey when you meet with them? Do your team members feel free to express their opinions and openly communicate with you?

3. Allow people to give you honest feedback on your behaviour. When was the last time you allowed someone to tell you how it is? They key here is to not punish them when they give you the feedback you have been asking for.

4. Park your ego and take the feedback on board. Don't take offence and keep it in your black book to use against them later on. To do this you have to be comfortable and secure in who you are. The best leaders/team members are those who don't have to prove anything and aren't driven by their ego. Practising this is a huge opportunity for growth.

5. Collect some formal feedback from those around you in the form of a survey. (Obviously this is more suited to the workplace. Your friends and family will give you strange looks if you survey them.)

BE VULNERABLE

In 2011 I was asked to speak at the managers' conference for Fuji Xerox. I was setting up to present when a well-dressed man with glasses bounded up to me.

'Hi, I'm Nick. I'm looking forward to your presentation this morning!'

I wondered how he could have so much energy at 7.30am. We talked about what I would be presenting that day, and he asked me lots of questions. I hoped the rest of the group would be as engaging and charming as he was. As the conference kicked off my energetic friend stood up and addressed the group. He was the managing director, Nick Kugenthiran, the man whose name I had practised the day before because I wanted to get the pronunciation right. I felt so embarrassed that I hadn't put two and two together. The sad part was that I hadn't thought he was the managing director because he was so much friendlier and more approachable than many of the MDs I had worked with in the past.

The conference was amazing. There was a fantastic buzz in the room. It was a pleasure to present to them. One of the highlights of the day was the video that the leadership team had put together of their bloopers when they were filming a corporate video. The audience roared with laughter and Nick starred in many of the out-takes. After meeting all the executive team, what struck me about them was how approachable and real they were. There was a severe lack of ego in this organisation.

Two weeks later, I was speaking at an education conference when two women approached me. They remembered me from the Fuji Xerox managers' conference (they were at the education conference as sponsors of the event), and we chatted. I asked why they thought the company was performing so well. They very quickly said, 'Because the leadership team is amazing. They've really nailed it with the people they have chosen.'

They then went on to tell stories of how the leadership team didn't see themselves as above the rest of the organisation. They mixed with all the employees and had deep, strong relationships throughout the company. They finished by saying, 'Because Fuji Xerox Australia has this sort of culture, it's a pleasure to work for them.' Following this, I asked a number of the education conference attendees what it was like to deal with Fuji Xerox Australia as a supplier. The comments were glowing. They talked about the prompt and helpful service they received from them and that their brilliant solutions helped the educators be more efficient.

After this interaction, I phoned Nick to give him the amazing feedback and also to interview him on the secret to his cultural success.

'When I moved into a senior role (where I was reporting to the MD) for Fuji Xerox Australia, I got used to making all the decisions,' Nick said. 'I got caught up and absorbed in myself. I had all the answers and was waiting for people to come to me so I could blow them away with my ability. One year into the role I was really struggling to manage family life and work life. So I started to reflect on how I was behaving as a husband and father. This led me to think about how I behaved at work and treated the people in my team. Luckily I was sent on a management course where I received 360-degree feedback from my leader, my peers and my team.

'After the 360-degree feedback the people running the course put some of the feedback up on the wall from across the team. Some of mine were up there: "Always finishes my sentences." "He will ask a question but answer it before we can say anything." "He is not interested in other people's input."

'I stood up in front of my team, pointed to the feedback and said, "Does anyone in the room know who this person is?" They all cringed, thinking it may be one of them. But I said, "It's me. I want to work on getting rid of these behaviours and I need your help to do that."'

Nick showed that he was vulnerable and ready to confront the changes that he needed to make.

'Since that day I have gotten over myself. I realised I was not perfect and it was important to let the rest of my team know. Three times a year we get together for a 'community in management' meeting where we talk about the organisation, what we will focus on moving forward and what we have achieved. I very much make it about the people in the organisation and what they have done to make the organisation great. In that forum I make sure that I stand up and share with them the mistakes I have made recently and what I have learned from them and how I will do better moving forward. This creates a culture where it is alright to say that we make mistakes, to acknowledge that and move on to correct it. It's about developing self-awareness. I am very comfortable getting up to share my failures. The reason I do it is because I want transparency and openness. If we don't confront and embrace our dysfunctions we can't change. The most important skill that a leader can have is the ability to be vulnerable.'

What is amazing about Nick's story is the business success that has come out of it. Commercially, this move has been an outrageous success. Fuji Xerox Australia has increased its value from a $700-million business to over a $1 billion business. In two years.

Nick continued. 'What I learned is that much more knowledge and capability lies around me. When it was just me, the insight was limited. However, when I allowed input from the people around me and accepted their contribution, our team really started to grow. Rather than thinking I had all the answers and trying to control everything, I gave up the power. If my direct reports all agree with me then that's not helpful. I need them to challenge me. When we have a board meeting we live in the left hand. The left hand is the conversation in your head that you think about but you don't say. I want to hear the left-hand conversations.

'What our leaders do now is, rather than being prescriptive to their staff about how they need to do the job, we have empowered people by telling them, "This is what we want to achieve. Go and find a way to achieve it."'

REAL LEADERS HAVE ENGAGED STAFF

Following this experience, I flew to New Zealand to present to Westfield in Auckland. I was particularly excited about this because my research showed that they had an engagement level of 84 per cent, which is almost unheard of and certainly one of the highest I have seen. The energy in the room was amazing; it was like a family reunion rather than a company office. I then got to meet the HR director who blew me away with her energy and enthusiasm. I spent some time watching her interact with the employees and she was joking around with them and winding people up for the start of the off-site. Then I met the managing director who was very friendly and authentic. He spoke about the organisation and you could sense his enthusiasm and passion for the people in it. Then I witnessed him be made fun of by his PA and other staff. You could tell that this was not an ego-driven, precious leader. He was part of the team.

Before I presented to the group the MD presented some awards. I was sitting next to two men from the construction division. One of the first awards was given to a man who had turned up on the day in a full suit and tie. He stood out because everyone else was in jeans and casual clothes. As he stood up for his award one of the construction men said to the other, 'I'm so glad that he got that award. He's such a nice person, really works his butt off.' All around me I heard similar things. No wonder their staff turnover was so low.

All organisations talk about the importance of respect and treating people with dignity. As leaders we know that we should be authentic and approachable. Unfortunately, too many leaders have this intention but their behaviour is completely different.

What these examples have in common is that the leaders' behaviour was congruent with their intention. The result was very high engagement levels and very low staff turnover. All this saved them huge amounts of money and kept their culture alive. I have worked in other organisations where the leaders viewed other people in the business with contempt and treated them as inferior. As expected, their engagement levels were lower and staff turnover much higher.

HOW TO CHANGE OUR BEHAVIOUR

In addition to being more aware of our behaviour and getting feedback about it, the second step is to work out the types of behaviours you want to exhibit.

I was conducting a full-day workshop with around 50 senior HR directors. The workshop was about behaviour change. I asked each of them to write down a change that they wanted to see in their organisation. They were able to do this very quickly and in fact many of them complained that this change was not a reality. I then asked them to articulate what were the exact behaviours that the people in the organisation needed to exhibit for that change to be a reality. Only two out of the 50 could actually come up with clear behaviours. Most of the responses, though, were very vague.

One woman's organisation introduced a new workflow system. I asked her, 'So what are the clear behaviours you want to see exhibited by the team?' 'Well, the team has to get on board!' she replied. I asked 'What does getting on board look like, how do I get on board?'

'They just have to be engaged with the new system.'

At this point, I stopped the workshop and drew everyone's attention to this. I pointed out that they complained about people in their organisations not changing, yet they couldn't tell these people how they needed to act for that change to happen. We do the same things with our health ('I need to eat better and exercise more'). We do the same to our partners. We complain about them not being attentive enough or nice enough to us, but when they ask us what exactly we want them to do, we are lost for words. For change to occur, we must clearly identify the behaviours we need to exhibit.

FOCUS ON BEHAVIOURS, NOT OUTCOMES

A big breakthrough in goal achievement came when researchers discovered that our chance of achieving a goal was greatest when that goal involved clear behaviours. One of the biggest blocks to behavioural change is that we set outcomes not goals. For example, one common goal in society is to lose weight. You may set a goal to lose ten kilograms in the next three months. It fulfils the usual metrics we use to measure the quality of our goals: it's specific, you can measure it, it's attractive, and it's most likely realistic and time-lined. However, this is a terrible goal. In fact, it's not a goal. It's an outcome.

The problem here is that there are no clear behaviours outlined. Specific behaviours that will get you this outcome are: exercising for one hour in the morning on Monday, Wednesday and Friday; skipping dessert; not drinking alcohol during the week and limiting yourself to two drinks on weekends; and keeping no sweets or junk food in your home. These are clear behaviours. Once you articulate these clear behaviours you greatly increase your chance of doing them and thus losing those ten kilograms.

You have now identified the behaviours you need to exhibit. As you transition, you want to keep that behaviour at the front of your mind. You want to visualise it. Athletes do this often. A common technique used in sports psychology is visualisation, also known as mental rehearsal or guided imagery. This is where you create a mental image of how you want to behave. You run through the behaviour you want to exhibit in your head. Athletes use this technique by picturing the race ahead. They visualise what will physically be happening, how they are performing, how it feels and what is happening around them.

When practising visualisation, you should focus on four senses: what you see, how you feel, what you smell and what you hear. For example, a swimmer preparing for a race will picture themselves on the blocks. They feel loose and relaxed, calm and composed. They imagine the roar of the crowd and smell the chlorine of the pool. They will visualise crouching down to take off. They picture themselves nailing the start, leaving right on the gun and springing off the blocks like a leopard, effortlessly. They enter the water and begin to stroke. They picture themselves swimming powerfully and gliding effortlessly through the water. They feel strong, they are swimming fast but staying loose and relaxed. Their stroke is perfect and fluid. As they head for the finish, they picture the other competitors slowing down as they accelerate and leave them behind. As they touch the wall in front they feel the emotion of elation and the crowd goes mad.

Research shows us that mental rehearsal significantly improves people's physical and psychological reactions to situations. In 1995, Dr Alvaro Pascual-Leone, professor of Neurology at Harvard Medical School, took a group of volunteers who had never played the piano and divided them into three groups. The first group was seated in front of a piano but not allowed to play. The second group learned a series of five piano finger exercises and practised them. The third group sat at the piano and was asked to visualise playing the piano.

After five days all study participants underwent a brain scan. The first group showed no change in their brains. The second and third groups showed identical changes in their brain structure. In other words, as far as the brain was concerned, imagining the task of learning piano was as good as doing the real thing.

As we transition can we visualise how we want to behave, what type of leader, parent or partner we want to be? If you have a challenging day ahead, can you walk into work visualising the behaviours you need to display to help you make it a success?

I was working with a manager who had moved from a company that had a high performance culture to a company that was struggling with a dysfunctional culture. I asked him how he was handling that transition. He said, 'I'm finding that people in this organisation tend to have a victim mentality where they complain about things rather than rolling up their sleeves and getting stuck into it. It's been making me quite stressed and angry, which has an impact on my health and personal life. When I showed up to work, my thoughts would be, "Here we go again. I can't stand these people; all they do is complain and moan and fight and carry on all bloody day."'

I asked him what he thought he could do to alter his response.

'I have to accept the fact that I can't change anyone, that all I can do is control my behaviour and set an example for my team.'

When we caught up a week later, he said, 'I know it sounds silly but I now picture as I walk in that I'm "Iron Man", and all the negativity just bounces off me; I'm immune to it. I think to myself, "I'm going to be proud of the way I've acted today." I picture myself being very calm and I picture myself being empathetic towards my co-workers. It has made a huge difference to my work. I make it a competition with myself as to how calm I can stay. I have my up days and some down days but not many. I have actually noticed that the behaviour of the team has changed a little. They still have a long way to go but through my example they are getting a lot better.'

Our behaviour affects the people around us. How we show up at work affects everyone around us and has an impact on the culture. All too often I see people complain about the culture of their workplace, yet they show up in a way that only reinforces that culture.

KEYS TO ENGAGING PEOPLE

Having worked with hundreds of organisations, these are the behaviours we can exhibit in the workplace that will universally improve the engagement of the people around us. While these are written with a business slant, you can apply the principles to all relationships.

Thank people for doing a good job. This is the simplest yet most effective thing you can do for your team. A manager I was working with introduced this into his team. He called me and said it has had the single biggest impact on his team compared to all other techniques. Initially his team thought something was wrong. Over time, however, he has seen a dramatic increase in engagement.

Get in their hearts and minds. This does not mean you have to sit down with your team every day and have tea and sticky buns. Are you generally interested in their welfare? Do you know what's happening in their lives? In a nutshell, do you give a damn about them as human beings?

Show them how they contribute to the company and make a difference. Recruitment company Randstad, in their 2010 'World of Work' report, found that one of the biggest motivators to perform well in the workplace was 'a strong understanding of how my role contributes to achieving organisational goals'. Humans have a strong desire to contribute and be part of something bigger than themselves. Show them how they make a difference.

Show them that their opinions count. When a member of your team expresses an opinion do you brush it off or do you pay it respect? When a person expresses an opinion, s/he is making themselves vulnerable. An essential part of leadership is to treat any opinion with respect and consider it, or at least discuss why it is appropriate or not appropriate. In our company, when we implement a strategy or plan something, we get every person's feedback on it.

Upskill your team. Do you send your team on training courses? Do you get them to hear inspiring presenters? Do you allow them to network with people in similar positions? A friend of mine, Peter Sheahan, is a very successful business consultant. He told me a story where a manager once said to him, 'I don't send my staff on training. What if I train them up and they leave?' Peter replied, 'What if you don't train them and they stay?'

Show them how they are improving. A sense of achievement and a feeling that we are moving forward is a key driver of happiness. People are more engaged and motivated when they can regularly see that they are improving.

As mentioned previously, many organisations and people talk a good game but act in an incongruent way. Here are two examples of organisations who aligned their intention with their behaviour.

CREATE SUCCESS FOR OTHERS

Ian Lynass is the CEO of a very successful company called BIS that supplies equipment to the mining industry. The clear intention of this company is 'creating success for others'. It is their core value. Throughout his career, Ian discovered that he became successful when he created success for those who reported to him by helping them understand themselves better, be the best they could be and achieving what was important to them. He realised that in isolation he couldn't be successful. He only achieved success through other people. While this may sound logical on paper, it's an entirely different thing to do it in practice. People often see their direct reports as competition, and while managers want their team members to do a good job, they might not want them to do too good a job. The mentality of helping those below you achieve is hard to inject into an organisation.

The entire culture of BIS has been built around the intention of making the people in lower ranked positions successful. Other companies have talked about similar aspirations but they rarely follow through with it. The reason it has worked at BIS is that the employees have aligned their behaviour to this intention. When you talk to the managers they never say that they are developing their people. They say they are creating success for their people. When new people join the organisation they are psychologically assessed, not to see if they are suitable for the job, but so the organisation can understand them better. When an employee starts at BIS, they come to Ian's head office within the first week. They meet everyone face-to-face.

They sit down with their managers and create a performance development plan both on a personal and business level, with targets and goals in it. This is then used as the template for them to be performance managed and measured against. Every six months each staff member comes back to review the plan. Instead of the manager running the performance review, the staff member actually provides the report to his or her manager. At the end of this, they reflect on the previous six months and then plan out the next six months to achieve what they want to be successful at.

To enable their intention even further, Ian inverted the organisation. The reality is that BIS makes money off the back of the workers out 'in the field'. They refer to the front-line employees who meet clients face-to-face as 'fighter pilots'. Ian's view is that everyone else in the organisation is a support infrastructure for the fighter pilots. He introduced a cultural attitude of 'we exist to make the fighter pilots more successful'. Put simply, if you're not helping a fighter pilot every day and helping them be more successful, BIS doesn't need your role.

What it means is that everyone in this organisation is measured on their ability to make the people below them more successful. Ian's fighter pilots are his executive team. He reaches out to them every day to make them successful. Their fighter pilots are equivalent to the general managers of the different business units. Everyone in BIS consistently asks themselves, 'What have I done to help a fighter pilot today?'

This philosophy has led to a very successful commercial organisation and engagement levels of the staff are very high. Ninety-nine per cent of open vacancies for senior roles are filled internally and they have a very low level of staff turnover. It's a beautiful example of an organisation tying clear behaviours to intention.

I asked Ian how he dealt with staff members who got caught up in their own ego instead of focusing on success for others? He replied, 'It's simple. All you do is show them that their success lies somewhere else.'

BIS had an intention to give back to the Indigenous community in Australia. Many companies in this space talk about giving back to the Indigenous community but very few get it right.

One of the challenges that the Indigenous community faces is lowlevel offenders (stealing, traffic offences) getting stuck in the criminal system. The rate of repeated offences in this group is huge because there are very few options for these men and women when they are released from prison. This leads to an escalation of seriousness of crime.

BIS started a 24-week training program for Indigenous offenders in jail (they leave the jail every day to attend the training). They receive training in cross-cultural skills, life skills, social skills and technical skills, so that when they are released, they are immediately qualified to work at BIS.

Ian welcomes them into the program on day one, and they are given a uniform with the BIS logo on it so that they are welcomed into the BIS family (not just the program). If they complete the program, BIS guarantees to employ them. If they don't attend the program or misbehave, they go back to jail.

When they are employed, they are not treated any differently to any of the other employees.

The workers coming out of the program are performing very well and some are the most skilled workers BIS employs.

This type of program has never been done before in Australia. Not only is it helping the Indigenous community but it has also improved the culture of BIS. Everyone is so proud of it. If you ask a BIS employee what is great about working for BIS, the community program is one of the first stories they will tell you.

THE CAMP OF HIGHEST QUALITY

As I walk into the foyer I am greeted by bright feature walls and up-beat music. It seems like a funky place to work, but to tell you the truth I've been to many funky offices. What really stands out is the huge whiteboard covered in handwritten messages: 'I nailed the budget', 'My sister had a gorgeous baby boy', 'I did the proposal in record time.'

As I walk through the organisation I notice that each person has a whacky photo of themselves up on their wall, and what must be a list of signature strengths. I walk into the office of Simon Rountree, the CEO of Camp Quality, and am greeted by a very fit-looking, relaxed man. After we shake hands he offers me his business card. He then pulls out a yellow card with two big holes in the bottom, at which point he slides his fingers into the card so they stick out like legs and he walks the card across the desk to me. I have to say that this a first, and the look on my face must be reflecting my thoughts. Simon interjects, 'Our theme at Camp Quality is that laughter is the best medicine. Therefore, we look for any opportunity to inject some fun into everything we do.'

Camp Quality is a very successful charity whose overarching purpose is to help children and families who are affected by childhood cancer. Their support exists in many different forms, from education and one-on-one support, to financial assistance and camps where the parents get a break and the kids have an absolute ball. Camp Quality is there with the kids and families every step of the cancer journey. Having been a Camp Quality volunteer for ten years, I've seen how hard this journey can be.

But I was not there to reminisce. A number of senior business leaders who knew I was writing this book told me to interview Simon as they rated him as an inspiring and unique leader. I was particularly excited because this was an organisation where the people in it have to go through massive amounts of transitions. This is a charity trying to raise money, which means it's constantly juggling a multitude of tasks on a small budget. On top of this, it's a charity that deals with, on a daily basis, distraught parents who have just found out that their child has cancer.

'At Camp Quality, we're not delusional optimists, we're realistic optimists,' Simon said. 'We have some pessimists in our organisation and that is actually important. We don't want our finance manager to be blindly optimistic. She needs to have an element of pessimism, she needs to look out for red flags. What we do have is a resilient attitude that leads to solution-focused thinking. As an organisation, we don't look at a glass and ask if it's half-full or half-empty. We look at a glass that is half-empty and ask, "Can we fill that glass up?" We make the glass full by 'choosing our attitude', we upskill the people in this organisation to deal with challenges, setbacks and knockbacks. Fun is crucially important to how they think and their attitude to life. Given that you spend so much time at work you should bloody well love it. To enable that to happen, we at Camp Quality have key behaviours we live by.'

Camp Quality's key behaviours are:

Having fun

Every staff member has a photo above their desk of themselves doing something silly. It reminds them not to be so serious. They also have a fun-therapy champion whose job is to ring a bell randomly once a week. When the bell is sounded, everyone has to stop for ten minutes and participate in a fun activity (past examples include a trivia quiz, paper aeroplane competition and playing marbles). Even if the leader of a big company is visiting the Camp Quality office s/he must go to the fun activity as well. While it's compulsory to attend, Camp Quality doesn't make it compulsory to get involved, as it can be confronting for new people. Simon pointed out that people usually can't help themselves. They see the excitement, the laughter, the joy, the connection that people are having, and they feel compelled to join in. It's just one human being enjoying the company of another human being. The feedback from the staff is that when they go back to work they are more productive than if they had stayed at their desks.

Camp Quality staff look for any opportunity to make a difference and make people smile and feel happy. Take, for example, the exchange of a business card. Instead of simply handing it over, they will place their fingers in it and make people smile. Simon said, 'I noticed that when I walked the business card over to you, you smiled and laughed. In a simple transaction like that I made a difference to you and made you feel better. In every interaction we inject a fun behaviour to make a difference.'

I noticed that every staff member has a desk calendar that sets them behavioural challenges. On Monday, it has the title 'Who can you make laugh today?' Each person in the organisation literally chooses someone and sets out to make them laugh at some point in that day. On Tuesday the title is, 'Focus on using one of your signature strengths.' On this day they look to incorporate their sig nature strengths into their working day. This desk calendar is another opportunity to reinforce behavioural habits that improve the culture and service of Camp Quality. Having these things there every day is a reminder to them to implement these behaviours. Over time it becomes second nature.

Choosing your attitude

At Camp Quality they believe that you and you alone have the ability to determine what the day will be like. The type of day you will have is a result of your attitude. They are not delusional; they recognise that the day ahead may be a really hard day, but it's about making the best of it and knowing that it will end at some point. The staff in Camp Quality deal with really difficult situations every day. They deal with grieving families, families that have to live near the hospital while their child gets treatment, and families that are so overwhelmed they don't know what to do next. The staff members realise this and know that the only thing they can do for the families is to be at their best, and the way they do this is by choosing the right attitude.

Displaying resilient behaviour

Simon gave an example of a recent day where they had been working on two very important and lucrative proposals to two corporate organisations. They had invested a huge amount of time and resources into it and it was a huge opportunity to get a significant donation. Both deals fell through on the same day. The team was rightly devastated. Simon sat down with them and said, 'Guys, this sucks. This is a huge disappointment. Will this be the demise of CQ? Are we going to fold?' 'No,' was the reply. 'We tried our best, they said the proposal was brilliant and spot on, but the decision was made beyond our control. They have financial pressures that we can't possibly influence. We're not going to lose our jobs over it.'

The team then celebrated the fact that they had done such a great job. They reflected on the companies' feedback, that these were some of the best proposals they'd ever seen. The team chose to be resilient rather than wallow in self-pity.

Focusing on signature strengths

Twice a year, all the staff members undertake a signature strengths test. Camp Quality uses this to manage and engage their people. They even alter people's job descriptions to suit their signature strengths. They don't spend time and money on training people on what they are bad at, they let the team use what comes naturally to them. Knowing other people's signature strengths has led to better communication and management within the organisation.

Being grateful

This behaviour is very much about living in the now – being thankful for today, being respectful of the past but not worrying about it and not being overly concerned about the future, which they can't control. One challenge that CQ faces is the tightening of the global economy and general decrease in the support of charity. These factors are beyond their control. They merely need to look at what they can control and be grateful for the opportunity of being able to try. Appreciate the day! At the end of the day each person writes down three things that they are grateful for on the desk calendar.

Celebrating victory

Camp Quality has a whiteboard in the foyer of every office (the whiteboard I noticed on the way in) where every staff member and visitor has to write a positive or happy message about anything as they leave the office. This practice ensures that the last thing that every person who leaves CQ thinks of is something happy or positive. At 5.15pm someone who works for CQ might get a phone call from a parent saying, 'My child has just been diagnosed with cancer and I don't know what to do.' Simon doesn't want them to walk out of the organisation with that weight as they go home. Writing on the whiteboard is a small jump-start to thinking positively. They also found that it was an amazing communication tool. If someone writes on the wall, 'My sister had a baby', people take notice and seek that person out to congratulate them. It breaks down silos within teams. If someone writes about bringing a new sponsor on board, everyone recognises and celebrates that victory. Unfortunately, the typical culture in a company is quite cynical. I think we live in a cynical society. The corporate world is driven by the bottom line. It's all about profit.

However, the above behaviours enhance the bottom line. When Simon took over Camp Quality it was on the brink of financial collapse. Now they raise $14 million each year. The staff has grown from 20 to nearly 90. Their program delivery has grown from three to seven programs. Volunteers went from a few hundred to now over 3000. The number of families they support went from around 1000 to over 5000. The numbers in their bottom line suggest that what they are doing with their culture is the right thing.

What I love about this organisation is that their behaviour is so tightly aligned with their intention. Many organisations talk about having this sort of culture. What Camp Quality does differently is incorporate simple, practical things into the environment to ensure that these behaviours are driven through the day. Simon says that it's all too easy not to do this stuff, and that the key is to firstly keep it simple. Secondly, it's important to continually remind people of the behaviours until it becomes a natural habit.

Some people may read this and think that it's easy to have that culture because they are doing something as meaningful as helping children with cancer. Simon believes that they would still have the same culture even if they were making widgets.

In fact, the Camp Quality culture has spread beyond its walls to make another organisation successful. The Canterbury Bulldogs NRL team has an amazing history and is a hugely successful club. However, the decade of the 2000s was an interesting one for the club – salary cap breeches and serious allegations around the off-field behaviour of the players left it a club that few sponsors wanted to be associated with.

The 2008 season was one that many would like to forget. They came stone, motherless last. Their star player walked out midseason and their sponsors were also looking for a back door to get out. One good thing that did happen was that they got a new CEO: the fresh-thinking and determined Todd Greenberg. He came to see Simon and asked him to form an alliance for signage on the jersey. Simon knocked him back, asking why he would accept such an offer when the Camp Quality brand was so good while theirs was busted. But Todd did not quit. He asked Simon how he built such a brand, to which Simon replied, 'Because of our culture.' Todd asked Simon if he could teach the Camp Quality culture to the Bulldogs.

Simon agreed on one condition: he must get access to all the Bulldogs staff. Coaching staff, players, admin staff, everybody. He agreed to run workshops with them all, but if the entire organisation did not embrace the culture, he would pull the pin.

Camp Quality literally taught the players and organisation the behaviours listed above. The Bulldogs went from last in 2008 to finishing one game off the grand final in 2009. Their membership started to climb. But the best result was the massive improvements in off-field behaviour that the players exhibited. They went from a toxic organisation that no one wanted to touch, to a shining example of what is possible. When asked how, Todd said that the tipping point was Camp Quality.

Who says that showing up with a clear intention and behaviour to back that up doesn't make a difference?

Camp Quality achieved success by being super clear on the behaviours they needed to exhibit, and ensuring that they drove those behaviours through everything they did.

SUMMARY

- While many of us have good intentions, the challenge is ensuring that our behaviours match those intentions.
- We all have dysfunctional behaviours that do not serve us.
- Unfortunately, many people are not aware of these dysfunctions and behaviours.
- The challenge is to be self-aware of these behaviours and understand their impact on other people.
- Having dysfunctional behaviours does not mean you are a bad person.
- Be transparent and open with people about the behaviours you need to work on. Get their support and input.
- Know the behaviours you want to exhibit and set up your environment to enable those behaviours.

Chapter 11

The Second Space

We have made it through the Third Space and come out the other side where we have entered the Second Space. If, for example, we are talking about leaving work and arriving home to our loved ones the final step of our journey is to ensure that the work we have done in the transition home is relevant and suited to the context of the home environment. When you enter the Second Space you have to ask yourself two questions:

1. Do I have an intention or an expectation?
2. Is my intention relevant?

INTENTION VS EXPECTATION

We often don't show up with an intention. We show up with an expectation. Expectations are set beliefs about the future. 'My staff will do exactly as they're told'; 'My partner will have dinner on the table for me each night when I get home'; 'People at work will speak to me with respect and courtesy at all times.' Expectations make us inflexible. They also set us up for frustration because the rest of the world didn't get the memo marked 'Urgent! Read now!' on 'How to act towards me at all times.' Most of our expectations are quite delusional and only set us up for pain. Lots of it. Look at road rage. When you get angry at people on the road your expectations are, 'No one is allowed to impede me on the road,' or, 'No one is allowed to make a mistake on the road.' Completely delusional.

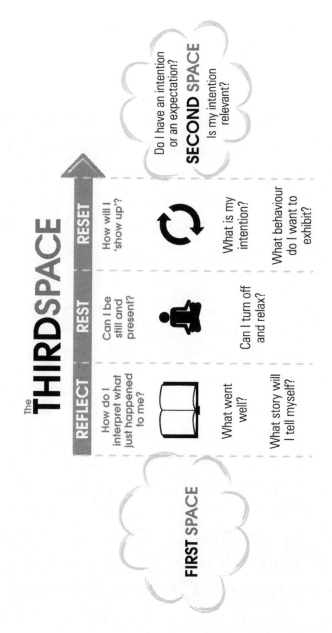

Expectations are dangerous because they are fixed; we get attached to them. One way to identify if we have an expectation rather than an intention is to look at the language being used. We often have fixed language attached to an expectation; in particular, words such as 'must' and 'should'. Expectations are also often to do with another person's behaviour, rather than our own. An expectation that people should be courteous on the road at all times will lead to road rage. In contrast, intention is a resolution to act in a certain way or achieve a certain outcome. For example, 'I will remain calm on the road despite what the people around me do,' is an intention. Intentions are far more flexible than expectations. The only thing you can control is your intention. You can't control other people's behaviour (trust me, I've tried). My wife will squeeze from the *top* of the toothpaste tube, no matter how many times I prove to her it's not the most efficient way.

You might transition into work with an expectation that your manager will treat you with respect, strive to engage you and not make mistakes. This expectation may leave you feeling frustrated and angry, as s/he may not live up to your expectation. Setting an intention of 'I will communicate with my manager in a clear manner, have empathy for them and respond to challenges by remaining calm' is an intention that will serve you much better. A psychologist once said to me, 'Sadness is the difference between expectation and reality.'

One of the most popular people I have ever met is a friend of mine called Monique. What makes her so popular is the fact that she never has fixed expectations of people. Friendships can sometimes break down because of the following expectations:

- They must call me and make an effort.
- If they are a good friend they will give me support when I need it.
- I shouldn't have to ask them for help, they should offer it.
- They should always invite me to social outings.

Monique never has expectations of her friends. When I asked her about this she said, 'Who am I to expect people to act a certain way? My focus when I am with my friends is to have the most fun possible and not judge. I focus on enjoying the moment. I can't control their behaviour but I can control how I behave when I'm with them.'

When I first became a parent, my intention upon transitioning home was to be a thoughtful and caring father. But with that, I carried an unreasonable expectation. When Bella flung her food on the floor or threw a tantrum I would get upset. My expectation was that she would behave in a reasonable, logical manner and not throw her food on the ground. Good luck with that, genius. She's 18 months old. My expectations were getting in the way of my intention. During that time, I had a meeting with a child-care worker and I expressed my frustration to her. She very nicely told me to get over myself and pointed out that kids are unreasonable and throw things all over the house. She said that if I had that expectation, fatherhood was going to be a tremendous struggle. I changed my intention to being a calm, loving and forgiving father, regardless of Bella's behaviour.

A friend of mine is a high performer. She owns a hugely successful company, has two degrees, is incredibly charming and excels at sport and pretty much anything she turns her hand to. Her husband is exactly the same. I was talking to her one day about parenthood and the expectations we have for our children. She told me that she and her husband had recently found out that their eldest child had a learning disability that meant that he'd never be able to study at university or have a job that requires the linking of complex concepts. With the pair of them being so incredibly successful, they had naturally thought that he would follow in their footsteps. She said the hardest thing about this situation is letting go of those very concrete expectations they'd had for his future.

IS MY INTENTION RELEVANT?

If we successfully use the Third Space, when we enter the Second Space we come in with a clear intention and an idea of the clear behaviours we want to exhibit. This helps us get into the right mindset for the next space. However, the Second Space is where reality comes into it, presenting us with a new role/task/environment. While it's great to be prepared once we enter the next space, we have to determine whether that intention is relevant. You might 'show up' to your desk with the intention of reorganising your files, when actually your intention should be to complete that proposal you have been putting off. When you add people into the Second Space, things start to get complicated. We are complex creatures and when you put a bunch of us together, the complexity grows exponentially. And the higher the stakes or the stronger the connection we have with a person, the greater the level of complexity.

You may 'show up' to a meeting with your team where your intention is to give them a clear strategy and pump them up. The behaviour you need to bring in order to outline a clear action plan is to be energetic and actively listen to their feedback and questions. But when you come into the room you discover that you've lost one of your big accounts and the team is devastated. At this moment, your intention needs to change. Your new intention is to stop them from falling into a pessimistic mindset and wallowing in self-pity, to help them look at the solutions and to have them walk away with a sense of possibility. Your new behaviour is to empathise with them, listen to them, be caring, stay positive and facilitate a discussion around how they can recover and move forward.

Sometimes as I'm coming home after work my intention is to be relaxed, fun and engaged with the family. I may have an expectation of being greeted at the door by my wife, glowing in her twin-set and pearls, with freshly baked muffins in the background. However, some days I am greeted at the door by Kathy Bates from *Misery* who hands me our daughter and says, 'I need you to take your child.' The 'your child' line is a giveaway that Chris has had a very tough day. At that moment, my previous intention is redundant. I have to shift it to a new intention that suits this space. I need to focus on how I can support her, make her life easier and give her time to relax. My behaviour becomes asking what she needs right now from me, and listening to her day without judgement or offering advice. It may be that what I need to do is look after Bella by taking her to the park so Chris gets 45 minutes to herself. Every space you move into you must ensure that your intention is relevant in that context.

My business manager and I were meeting with a client following the wrap-up of a retainer arrangement they had engaged me on. We had planned the meeting and had a very clear intention: to show them the benefits for the leadership team to extend the program. Our behaviour was around further under-standing their needs and how we could help. When we walked into the meeting we could tell that our client was having the day from hell. She looked exhausted, distracted and simply fed up. At this point, our original intention went out the window and our new one was to offer her support and simply reinforce the relationship we had with her. We spent the meeting talking about her current challenges; we empathised with her and lent a supportive ear. At the end of the meeting we said that it sounded like she had too much on to make any decisions about next year and suggested meeting again after the holidays. Our follow-up meeting went very well and we got our original intention. In the meeting, she told us how thankful she was that we didn't push her to make any decisions. She said it showed that we had a genuine interest in the relationship beyond money.

The key to understanding whether our intention is relevant is to understand the context of the Second Space. This is the ability to read other people and understand often complex social situations. It may range from a work meeting that has a political agenda to a family barbecue where two cousins are about to wage war on each other.

There are two key things we need to do to understand the context of any space we move into. We need to have empathy and we need to listen.

EMPATHY

Empathy is defined as the ability to recognise and relate to the emotional state of other people; to put yourself in someone else's shoes. Empathy is closely related to compassion. To feel compassion for another person, the first step is to have empathy for them.

I am constantly surprised at the lack of empathy I see, particularly in the workplace. Following the February 2011 earthquake, the city of Christchurch was devastated. Lives were lost, buildings were destroyed and essential services were disrupted. One of the biggest challenges the people of Christchurch faced were the thousands of aftershocks that followed. This made the population constantly on edge. People weren't sleeping, they were anxious and depression was rife. In the months following, I found myself in meetings or workshops with companies that had a Christchurch branch. A number of people exhibited frustration at the Christchurch office not getting up to speed quickly enough. One person said, 'I'm tired of Christchurch using the earthquake as an excuse. They need to step up and get on with it.'

It was terrible to witness this lack of empathy, understanding and compassion of an event that will affect the community for decades.

I did an assignment with a large telecommunications company in their call centre. The objective was to reduce the stress levels and emotional reactions of the call centre staff. I couldn't believe how hard their job was. They literally have people yell at them all day and often have to deal with very abusive callers. As a result, many of them return this abuse or get stressed and angry. This results in terrible customer service and a bad day for the staff member. During our workshop, we hooked up staff members to various instruments that measured their level of stress and we had them take live calls. We trialled various techniques like deep breathing and squeezing stress balls to reduce their level of stress and help them give a great customer experience. However, the most effective technique we found was having empathy for the caller. When the staff member genuinely wanted to understand the customer's frustration and solve their problem, they themselves became much calmer. And when the staff member empathised with the customer ('So sorry, sir. That must be incredibly frustrating for you,' or, 'I can see why you would be so upset about that'), the customer became so much calmer and friendlier. I was talking to a senior staff member in the call centre. He said, 'I have been working in call centres for 30 years. Most people who call don't expect to have their problem solved. They're just looking for someone to say, "That is really unfortunate that that happened. I am so sorry about that and I will see what I can do to fix it."'

We are so quick to judge people and so slow to empathise with them. Naturally our empathy gets better as we get older due to life experience and a capacity to relate to more situations. Every time you move into a new space, think about what is happening for the people in that space.

LISTENING

Active listening requires an attitude where we seek to understand the other person, not just drive our own point home. This is beyond being present (being present is the first step in listening); it's a mindset of understanding. Real listening is where you become attuned to the other person's feelings, letting them express their point of view and taking it on board. This massively builds rapport. Everyone wants to feel understood.

How do we become good listeners? There are many varied articles that tell us to do things such as mirror the other person's body language, ask open-ended questions, or create a conducive physical and mental space by removing distractions. I find many of these techniques inauthentic and trite. The reality is that if you want to be a good listener, you need to 'show up' with an intention to understand the other person. This will go a lot further with people than matching their physiology and keeping eye contact.

EMPATHY AND LISTENING CAN CHANGE HOW YOU 'SHOW UP'

Human resources (HR) is a role that requires multiple transitions. Because of the nature of the role, you are often transitioning in and out of incredibly delicate and emotional situations. Avril Henry is one of the foremost experts on the engagement and management of workforces. She has had a distinguished corporate career and now runs her own consultancy. The second part of Avril's corporate career was spent in HR, and when I ran the concept of transitions past her she outlined that in her time she had transitioned in and out of many stressful spaces, having dealt with cases of sexual harassment, bullying, fraud and even a death at a Christmas party.

Avril has had an interesting life. She grew up in a small mining town in South Africa, where women were not expected to do more than get married or become a bank teller. She was born into a family that didn't have a lot of money and didn't give a lot of emotional support to the children. From an early age, Avril was bright and ambitious and knew that she had a desire to go to university and have a better life. She worked out that in order to get there she would have to get a scholarship, but only one was given to each high school by De Beers. She studied with fury and passion and achieved her dream.

From this, she learned that all that matters is results. If you want something you have to work bloody hard for it to get those results. She also learned that when you got results you also got recognition and praise, something she craved in her home environment. Avril's life became all about getting results.

This attitude served her well in her chosen field of accounting. She described herself as a 'hard-arse accountant'.

'I never missed deadlines and I was ruthless about results. In fact, I would pursue results over relationships every day of the week. And then I was given an opportunity to move into HR.

'I took my "results at all costs" mindset into my HR role. I would give presentations about a particular HR issue to a group and tell them, "This is how you need to do it from now on. It's the law so you better get over yourselves and get it done."'

She said there was no engagement or inclusion in what she did. Because she was dealing with some very sensitive issues, this became a problem. Colleagues began to call her names behind her back, complaining that she was taking the fun out of the workplace.

'In finance you are very directive and assertive, often even aggressive. The numbers have to be right, but finance people tend to want to be right beyond the numbers.'

Even though Avril was getting amazing results, she was leaving a trail of disenfranchised people behind her. Her boss at the time called Avril on her behaviour in a performance review.

'Your weakness is that you set high standards for yourself and others but you punish them if they don't achieve it,' her boss told her. Avril was devastated.

She attended training workshops, read books and hired a coach in a bid to develop her empathy and listening skills. She learned the value of 'I' statements rather than 'you' statements. For example, 'When this happens I feel upset', rather than, 'You make me feel upset'. She learned the importance of being quiet and listening actively. She learned to control her emotional reactions. But most importantly she learned empathy for others.

'When you tell someone that they have to change something, whether it's a restructure, a new policy or a change in staff, they have an emotional reaction to it. This is the number one thing businesses get wrong – they don't take into account the emotional impact on the people.'

Today Avril is still focused on results, but she is also focused on relationships and has empathy for the people she deals with. She said that empathy and listening have given her the ability to look at different ways of solving problems and dealing with people.

SUMMARY

- When you 'show up' to the Second Space, ensure it is intention that is driving you, not expectation. Intention is flexible, while expectation is rigid.
- Check the context of each space to ensure that your intention is relevant.
- In order to do this, make sure you have empathy for the people in that next space and actively listen to them.

Chapter 12

Conclusion: making it work for you

There you have it! You have all the tools you need to effectively handle the micro-transition from one area of your life to another, thus resulting in greater balance and happiness. When you meet each of life's micro-transitions, remember to Reflect, Rest and Reset.

REFLECT

Every time you transition out of the First Space, take time to ask yourself if your story is *accurate, realistic* and *optimistic.* Ensure, too, that you remember to look at *what went well.* Reflect will help shift you into positive emotion, give you a sense of achievement and show you that you are actually progressing. This sets up a solid platform on which you can tackle what is coming next.

REST

Take the time to pause, allow yourself to be present and move forward with a clear, calm mind. Rest re-anchors and grounds you as well as prepares your brain to function at its best. Whether Rest lasts for 20 seconds or 20 minutes it's worth the effort. The benefits of this one will surprise you.

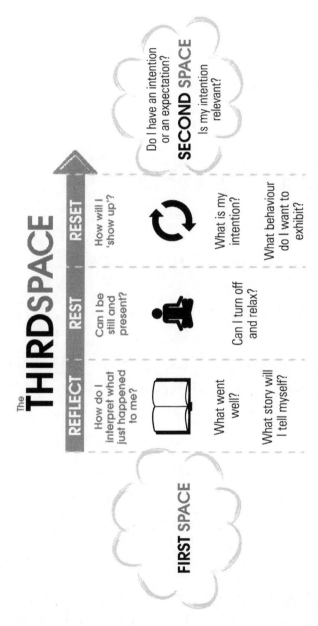

RESET

This is where you prepare to 'show up' for the all-important Second Space. Reset helps you clarify your intention for the next space and ensures that your behaviour aligns with this intention.

SECOND SPACE

Once you enter that next space, check that you are carrying an intention, not an expectation, and that your intention is relevant.

One of the challenges you may face in implementing this technique is that it may not feel big enough or drastic enough. But that is the beauty of it. Just like our elite tennis players that we discussed in Chapter 2, what separated the elite players from the good players was what they did in between the points. The great players were the ones who practised the Reflect phase on the previous point and 'got over it'. They had a short period of Rest where they calmed their physiology down to help them recover and conserve energy. Then, finally, they Reset for the upcoming point, where they would focus on intention with an optimistic mindset. While it may not make a big difference doing it for only one game, it certainly made a huge difference when done consistently over five sets. Similarly, Steve Hooker consistently did the small things day in and day out for four years to win a gold medal in pole vault at the Beijing Olympics.

CONSISTENCY IS KEY!

In his book *The Tipping Point,* Malcolm Gladwell discusses a theory called the 'broken window theory', first proposed by James Q. Wilson and George Kelling in 1982.[1] Put simply, the theory states that if a building had a broken window, it would send a message to the neighbourhood that nobody cared about the building, and that it was okay to break more windows. This mentality would then spread to the next building, and the next, until the entire neighbourhood was damaged. In other words, the theory suggested, crime is contagious and little things like this send a signal to people that it is okay to repeat that behaviour.

In the late 1980s, when New York was in the grip of a crime epidemic, its city officials adopted the broken window theory in various contexts. First, they looked into reducing crime on the subways. Two things were done. Firstly, David Gunn, new director of the subway system, focused on something seemingly small – stamping out graffiti. He saw graffiti as a broken window that signalled that it was okay to damage the trains. At the end of the line, each train was inspected for graffiti. If any was found it was immediately cleaned before being sent out again.

The theory was also adopted by the new director of the transit police, Willam J. Bratton. Rather than focus on violent crimes, he decided to focus on fare evasion. It was estimated that over 150,000 people each day were jumping the turnstiles. Even though it was a small crime, it sent a strong signal to others that it was okay to commit crimes on the subway. The transit police clamped down on this particular crime, arresting anyone avoiding the fare. They also began running background checks on each person caught, and quickly discovered that one in seven of them had outstanding warrants.

This focus on eradicating graffiti and fare evasion sent a powerful message to the public that such behaviour was not acceptable. The result? Subway crime plummeted.

I see the same thing in corporate cultures. Leaders talk about company values, but every time a behaviour that goes against those values is tolerated, it sends a signal to the rest of the company that they can act that way too. When a parent scolds their child for a particular behaviour, and then goes on to exhibit the same behaviour themselves, it tells the child that behaving well isn't really important. Going back to those micro-transitions, it's important that you practise the Third Space consistently. Every time you transition ineffectively and 'show up' poorly, you send yourself a signal that it's okay not to be accountable for your own behaviour.

It's the small elements of our behaviour that mount up and make a difference.

Using the Third Space consistently will make a huge difference in your life. Of course, I don't expect you to use every detail of the Third Space for every single transition you make in a day. That's just not realistic. But it's up to you now to make it fit into your world.

One executive explained to me how he uses the Third Space:

'I do the full thing – Reflect, Rest and Reset – every time I transition between something significant: between home and work, between meetings, between major tasks, between important interactions with people and finally as I transition home. However, regardless of what I am doing, every time I start something new I always ask myself "how am I showing up?" Even if I'm just sitting down at my desk to check emails or having a quick conversation with my assistant, I ask myself this.'

If you regularly practise this technique you will be more productive, resilient, focused, have greater self-awareness of your behaviour, be less stressed and have better relationships. Why do we want all of this? Three words: to be happy. If you were to ask anyone why they do what they do, and keep probing deeper and deeper, you will always get to the same answer: to be happy!

Why do you work so hard?

To provide for my family!

Why do you want to provide for your family?

So they can have great opportunities and a good life!

Why do you want them to have a good life?

It will make me happy.

Why do you work for a not-for-profit organisation?

So I feel like I am making a difference!

Why do you want to make a difference?

So that I feel like I have contributed to making the world better!

Why do you want to feel like you have made the world a better place?

It will make me happy.

Everything is about finding happiness.

In the last five years there has been an explosion in the research around what makes us happy. When you think about it, this is kind of sad – we are studying how to be happy.

Much of the research around happiness is showing that happiness is quite counterintuitive. Psychologist Ed Diener has essentially shown that in terms of our happiness, it is more important to experience frequent moments of happiness than more intense and infrequent events of happiness. In other words, you are better off having a number of small good things happen to you than one amazing event. This suggests that the small things do matter. If happiness is your goal, you need to endeavour to make each space a pleasurable experience rather than hold out for the one space that puts you on cloud nine.[2]

In support of this, Daniel Gilbert, a Harvard psychology professor, points out that very few experiences, both good and bad, have a lasting effect on us beyond three months. When an amazingly positive event happens, we celebrate it for a short while and then get on with life. Likewise, when something devastating happens, we take a hit, dust ourselves off and get on with the show.[3]

What this tells us is that to be happy we have to be happy in each space we move into. What researchers are also discovering is that the benefits of feeling positive emotions like happiness are reaching further than ever thought possible.

THE POWER OF POSITIVE EMOTION

Why do we have emotions? What is the point of them? Why were they given to us? Many people say they make us human, but it goes deeper than that. Our emotions:

CONTROL OUR MOTIVATION

Our desire to do something is controlled by the emotion we relate to that task. Have you ever set your alarm to get up early and exercise, yet stayed in bed? What emotion do you feel when the alarm goes off? Apathy, sadness, anguish, disgust, irritation. So you stay in bed. From here, you create your own logic and begin to justify why you should stay in bed. 'I've had a hard week and I deserve a lie-in.' 'Is that rain I can hear?' What kept you in bed? The negative emotions you associate with getting out of bed to exercise.

Compare this scenario to the day you have to be at the airport at 5.30am to fly to Italy for a holiday. How easy is it to get out of bed that day? You're up every hour shouting, 'Is it time to go yet? Should we get there four hours earlier to be safe?' The difference here is that the emotions you have attached to the overseas holiday are elation, happiness, excitement and enthusiasm.

I used emotion to get on track with my exercise regime. I love to lift weights but the thought of doing cardiovascular exercise (walking, running, cycling) makes me nauseous. In fact, I would rather stick bike spokes in my eyes, it's that tedious. However, it's obviously good for my health so I strive to do it. After reading about the role of emotion in exercise I thought about what types of cardio I *do* like. Swimming was the answer. So off I went to the local pool to power out some laps. Ten laps in, I found myself getting monumentally bored. I thought, is there any way I can inject some fun into my swimming? The solution: I joined a swim squad. Every morning at 5.45, we meet as a group and do a session with our coach. I love it. The people are great, and no session is the same because the coach changes it, so the time ends up passing so quickly. What's the difference? When I picture getting up for a swim, the emotion is positive and I am looking forward to seeing the people in the squad. The positive emotion is so strong that I'm able to show up to an outdoor pool in winter when it is a chilly four degrees outside.

How engaged you are at work depends on what emotions you feel in relation to the work you do and the people you work with. Your desire to go out and socialise with friends hinges on the emotions you feel when you picture going out. If it's dread, annoyance and misery, you will stay at home. It explains why shoving bamboo under your fingernails looks mildly appealing when you think about visiting the in-laws.

AFFECT OUR ENVIRONMENT

In Chapter 8, we discussed that our emotional state or our mood is contagious and affects the mood of the people around us. The emotions you show up with affect the emotion of that environment. I refer to this phenomenon as 'emotional influence', where your emotions influence the emotions of others. This emotional exchange is far-reaching, and people who are involved in a highly engaged conversation not only end up with the same mood as the other person but also begin to exhibit the same physiology – breathing rate, heart rate, body position and muscle tension.

A study conducted by the Institute for Social and Economic Research in 2011 showed that the biggest predictor of whether children were happy in the home environment was whether their mother was in a good mood. Sorry to put more pressure on you, mums.

This concept extends into the workplace. Daniel Goldman and Richard Boyatzis[4] have said that 'emotional intelligence (the ability to recognise and regulate emotion in ourselves and others) is carried through an organisation like electricity through wires'. They discovered that to guarantee a team's success, the leader needs to show up in an authentic, optimistic and high-energy mood. Through their actions, the team will show up that way too. Countless studies have shown that when a leader shows up in this state, the team starts to view things with a positive bias. Team members become more confident about their chosen goals; they are more creative and resourceful and are more helpful to each other.

A tyrannical and callous manager who 'shows up' to work with a mood of resentment, contempt and anger will create a mood of toxicity and dysfunction. His or her team will spectacularly underperform. Team members will begin to look for the problems in situations and develop a pattern of learned helplessness. They may begin showing up with a victim and persecutory mindset. Studies also tell us that a leader who uses fear to motivate their team will see an initially spectacular increase in results, but these do not last and will irreversibly kill the workplace culture.

But wait, there is good news! Sigal Barsade from Yale School of Management showed that positive emotions are more contagious than negative ones. Playfulness, warmth and cheerfulness spread through an organisation more easily than irritability and depression. Paul Eckman, the world's premier expert on facial expressions and their link to emotions, once told me that a smile is incredibly infectious. In fact he cited a study where a manager had to sack one of his employees. After he delivered the news, the manager smiled at the fired employee who could not help but smile back. As corny as it sounds, what your mum said was true: 'Smile and the world smiles with you.'

DRIVE OUR BEHAVIOUR

At a very basic level, the primary function of an emotion was originally to help us survive. Emotions can hijack the brain and cause us to react very quickly. So in effect the emotions we feel in a day drive our behaviour.

Have you ever bought something you didn't really need? Of course you have! You're standing in front of it, and the logical part of your brain starts to kick in. You don't need it, you can't afford it, it's not practical ... yet you walk out with it. Why? Because of the emotional kickback you feel from making the purchase. We are driven by emotions. It happened to me, too. I recently walked into the Apple computer store just after they had released the 11-inch MacBook Air (a small, extremely thin notebook computer). At the time, I had three laptops that all worked fine.

As I was looking at it, the salesman started to tell me about it.

'It is so thin you can post it in an envelope.'

Yeah, I thought. That's what I need from a computer, the ability to mail it.

I walked out with it. There was no logical reason why I needed that computer. I simply bought it because it was cool, and if it's cool, maybe I am cool. It was a purely emotional purchase.

Top salespeople often say, 'Logic makes them think, but emotion makes them buy.' Ponder this: if people were driven by logic rather than emotion, there would be no extra-marital affairs, no one would eat junk food, no one would smoke and there would be no road rage.

We buy products and join social networks because of the emotional kickback that occurs as a result. What is branding? The emotional attachment you have to a company, the emotion you relate to that company. This is why women pay $1000 for a pair of Manolo Blahnik shoes or $5000 for a Dolce&Gabbana handbag. It's not that they actually think it's a great price to pay for a handbag. They are compelled to buy it because of how it will make them feel to have those particular shoes or that specific bag.

An executive from Harley-Davidson once said: 'The company doesn't sell motorcycles. What we sell is the ability for a 43-yearold accountant to dress in black leather, ride through small towns and have people be afraid of him.'

Why do people buy Harleys? Because of how a Harley makes them feel! If you were buying a motorbike and you used logic, you would buy a

Japanese motorbike; you buy a Harley on pure emotion.

Emotions also drive engagement in organisations. Engagement is simply how an employee feels when they come into work. If they come in feeling enthusiastic, happy, excited and energised, they are engaged. If they come in feeling resentful, angry, frustrated and sad they are disengaged.

POSITIVE EMOTIONS LEADS TO SUCCESS

Research on happiness has shown that people who have aspects in their life, such as a functional relationship, comfortable income, good health and stimulating passions, tend to be happier than those who do not have these things. For many years it was thought that happiness and well-being were the results of those good things in their life. However, we now believe that this relationship may exist in the other direction. A group of scientists got together and examined the research around happiness, looking at more than 200 studies. They concluded that happy people (those who experience a large amount of positive emotions) tend to be successful and accomplished across multiple aspects of their lives, for the simple reason that positive emotion leads to better performance and success.[5]

Why do positive emotions lead to success?

For quite some time we have understood the role of negative emotion. Fear, anger and anxiety are all useful negative emotions in terms of our survival. Negative emotions help us stay cautious and safe, and thus alive. In contrast, the existence of positive emotions has confused and puzzled researchers. The answer, however, was found in Barbara Fredrickson's 'broaden and build' theory.[6] This theory shows that when a human being is in a positive state, he or she feels free from immediate danger and takes this opportunity to expand resources, build a repertoire of skills, and set new goals that have not yet been achieved.

In other words, when we are in a negative emotional state, our attention narrows, our creativity shrinks and we go into preservation mode. When we have positivity, we can relax, our attention expands, we become more creative and our brain starts to look at using this safe period to improve and evolve until the next period of preservation. Regular feelings of positivity put us in an 'upward spiral' of growth and we flourish. There is ample evidence to support this theory. Positive emotions incite people to be more creative, unifying and flexible in their thinking.[7]

It also helps people to be more measured in their responses, and more strategic and proactive in their behaviours.[8] Positive emotions have even been shown to increase our peripheral vision and allow the brain to take in more information to process, while the presence of negative emotions has the opposite effect and literally narrows the mind.[9] From an evolutionary perspective, this makes sense: when you're being chased by a beast that sees you as an entree, you don't want your brain to be thinking, wow, look at the pretty bird.

Regular experiences of positive emotion has been shown to lead to improved confidence, optimism, likeability, increased belief in your ability, positive perception of others, energy, immune function, health status, social ability, coping with stress, originality, creativity and flexibility.[10]

Even your performance at work can be improved by positive emotions. The emotional state of 272 employees was measured to determine their level of positive emotions. Eighteen months later, the researchers found that those employees who felt a high level of positive emotions had been promoted more, had better relationships at work, and enjoyed their work far more than employees who had a higher level of negative emotions.[11]

Our management skills are also profoundly improved by positive emotions. Managers who have a higher level of positivity are more precise and accurate in their decision-making process, and are also better at the interpersonal side of management.[12]

During a presentation to the senior leaders of a power station, I shared the latest research about positive emotions with them. The manager of the power station came up to me afterwards and said, 'That is really powerful stuff and so true. I'm going to make sure we address this at the power plant.'

A couple of months later I received an email from him thanking me for the workshop. He wrote that the executive team now gets together each morning for a 'mojo check-in'.

'A power station organisation, particularly, is heavily biased towards an engineering, technical, compliance, risk and transactional focus. We never talk about emotions or how we are coping. What we have started to do is get together as a leadership team each morning to see what our "mojo levels" are like. We literally stay in there until we are in a positive mood and then we go out and start our day. We know that each day our emotions affect everyone at the plant, so we use this little pause in the morning to ensure we go out and influence them the best we can.'

This mojo check is a way of using the Third Space to ensure that they have a positive impact on their culture.

In life, we all have to negotiate and try to get the best deal possible, whether it's a conversation with your boss about a pay rise, trying to get your child to go to sleep, or coming out ahead in a divorce settlement. A study was conducted to measure the impact of displaying positive, negative or neutral emotions on achieving one's desired resolution. The first experiment had people in a dispute situation. Those who exhibited positive emotions during the negotiation were more likely to keep the business relationship intact.

The second experiment was an ultimatum situation. The managers who exhibited positive emotions were more likely to close the deal. The study also showed that the other party was willing to pay more to someone who showed positive emotions than someone with negative emotions.

The final experiment was a distributive situation. The results showed that people who showed positive emotions received greater concessions from the other party. In contrast, the other party made far more extreme demands when met with someone who displayed negative emotions.[13]

Another study was conducted where the researchers set people up to feel positive emotions such as happiness, or negative emotions such as fear. What they found was that the subjects who were in a positive emotional state were able to come up with many more creative ideas and had greater attention focus.[14]

Positive emotion literally primes our brain to work on a more sophisticated, accurate and creative plane.

***

When I was 17 I learned the importance of having a creative and open mind. In that year, my best friend and I designed a board game. We were very excited about the idea and were certain that we would retire as millionaires at the age of 20.

Our self-belief was so great that we saved up all our money and had a prototype made. It looked incredibly professional and you could play it like a real board game. Being 17 and not yet knowing how the world worked, we started cold-calling executives in the toy industry. We just kept calling until one finally relented and said that he would meet with us. We caught the train up to Sydney from Wollongong and met the executive, who was in his early 50s, looking very dapper in his very expensive suit and silver hair. I was wearing stone-wash jeans and I had a mullet haircut. Hey, it was the early 1990s!

We laid out the board games and walked him through the whole concept.

'Look,' he said. 'I have to be honest. It's pretty good, but it won't sell and this is where it ends. But hey, a great effort for two young guys. Don't give up and keep trying.' As we were leaving I asked him what led him to say yes to the meeting.

He said, 'When I was working in the US, we would regularly have people come in and pitch ideas to the executive team. One day this guy walks in and says, "I have the next big idea; what happens is four turtles get flushed down a sewer, but when they fall in, they hit radioactive waste and mutate into teenage turtles.

Then they walk along the sewer and meet a rat. But he is no ordinary rat, he is a ninja master and he teaches them how to be ninjas. They're all named after famous artists, they each wear a different colour and they have different weapons. But the coolest part about the whole idea is they only eat pizza ... what do you think?"'

'We burst out laughing,' the executive said. 'We thought it was the dumbest idea we had ever heard. Years later, *Teenage Mutant Ninja Turtles* was the biggest thing on the planet and we missed out on billions. After that day I make sure I greet every idea with an open mind.'

I can't for the life of me remember the executive's name and I haven't any way to work out if that story he told us was true or whether he was yanking our chain. Either way, it's still a great story and illustrates a powerful lesson.

THIRD SPACE IN ACTION

TRANSITIONING INTO AN EXAM

A typical transition into an exam involves you getting highly stressed and focusing on how poorly prepared you are. You project the worst outcome and convince yourself that the exam will concentrate only on all those things you did not have time to cover in your study. As you stand outside the exam room, you read over your notes one last time in an attempt to cram as much information into your brain as you can.

When the other people in your course arrive, you start the pre-exam bitch session, where you all compete to see who did the least amount of study.

'I only glanced over my notes. I'm sure I will crash and burn in this exam big time.'

'You reckon you haven't studied much? I've done nothing.'

You sit down at the desk with a dry mouth and a rapidly beating heart. They put the exam paper in front of you, and then you begin to panic. Your mind races. You look at the first question and you vaguely remember reading something about that theory. 'Damn, if only I could remember! Better move on before I waste too much time on this one. Oh, no. I knew that would be on the exam. I think I missed that lecture...'

This is not a great way to transition into an exam if you want to have good performance. Let's rewind it back a bit.

You arrive to the exam room.

Reflect

When you arrive, rather than talking to other people, you spend the time reflecting on what you have been happy with about your preparation. You take time to reflect on previous exams that you have done well in and have felt comfortable with. You carefully choose to explain to yourself that you always perform well in exams and, in fact, you realise that you have never failed an exam, and in terms of preparation for this one, you're actually extremely well prepared.

Rest

When you sit down at your desk, you slow your breathing rate right down and focus your mind on a single spot on your desk. You simply empty your mind and enjoy the relaxed feeling.

Reset

When you are told to start writing, rather than attack the paper you take a moment to remind yourself of your intention. Your intention is to not panic at all but to stay calm during the next three hours and allow all the things you have learned to come out on the paper. You remind yourself of specific behaviours you are aiming for. Keep breathing deeply; when thoughts around doubting your ability come in you simply let them pass like trains passing through a station. Each time you feel your mind race and you get confused, you insert another period of Rest. You stop what you are doing, take a deep breath, and focus the mind on that single spot. Once you are calm you come back to the exam.

Reflect again

When you leave the exam, you avoid standing out the front and comparing notes on what you think you got right or wrong. All the way home you reflect on what you did well, how you remained calm and how you logically thought out a question you didn't immediately know the answer to.

Compare these two examples. In the first, notice how the brain is set up to fail and be ruled by negative emotion.

The second example incorporating the Third Space primes the brain to recall information and be creative. It allows the sophisicated part of the brain to hold onto and process the right information.

DATE NIGHT

You've had a day that you would rather forget. Tight deadlines, dysfunctional people focusing on petty turf battles and IT issues that meant half of your day was wasted. But that is history as tonight is date night. The kids are being looked after and your partner has organised for you to go out for a great meal and a relaxing evening together. You make a mad dash out of work because you are already running late. You're not entirely sure of the restaurant's location as you have never been there before. Rather than stop to print off a map, you decide to wing it. Friday night traffic is now heavy as usual, making you really late. In the back of your mind you can't stop thinking about someone in your team who is having a negative impact on your workplace culture.

As you get close to where you think the restaurant is your mobile rings. It's work! One of your direct reports is having trouble locating a file that they need for a presentation tomorrow. By the time you've talked them through it, you realise you missed your turn-off and have to do another loop through the city. Twenty minutes later you get to your original position. Where the hell is this place? You finally find the street but getting a park is another issue. You spend 15 minutes finding a park and then ten minutes walking to the restaurant. You're angry, sweaty, flustered and 75 minutes late. You are seated at the table and your partner gives you a look that says a thousand words. You explode.

'Don't start with me. I can't understand why you insist on choosing these stupid bloody restaurants that are out of the way and no one can find.'

Your partner snaps back. 'Well I was here on time.'

'That's because you can leave work whenever you want. I actually work for a living. I can't just run off at the drop of a hat...'

You know the rest of the story. Date night turns into silent night. Silent, prickly and uncomfortable night.

Let's rewind.

You race out of the office running late, but you pause to print off a map to ensure you know exactly where you have to go. Friday night traffic is a disaster as usual, but rather than get upset you slip in a favourite CD, text your partner that you are on your way and relax.

Reflect

As you are driving along you go over the day and reflect on what you have achieved. You choose to focus on the improved communication you have established with your direct reports. You are happy with how proactive you have become and the impact the greater clarity has had on the team's culture.

Upon this reflection, you recognise that your leadership has come a long way in the last 12 months and you feel pretty good about this.

As you come up to your turn-off, your mobile starts to ring. It's someone from work. You very quickly tell the person that you will call them back. You make your turn and start the search for an elusive park in the city. After 15 minutes you find one and start to walk to the restaurant. While you are walking you call the office back and identify the missing file.

Rest

When you get to the restaurant you are flustered and feeling rushed so you don't go straight in, you pause to take a couple of deep breaths. You reflect on how you are feeling and determine that you are feeling a little resentful about the fact that you've spent over an hour trying to get to this tiny, obscure restaurant. Add to this the fact that you are just plain exhausted.

Reset

You remind yourself of the intention behind date night: to enjoy each other's company and strengthen your relationship. You reflect on the behaviours you want to exhibit. You put yourself in your partner's shoes: they have been waiting nearly an hour for you to arrive, and may feel embarrassed or bored sitting alone in a restaurant. Therefore, the chance of them being cranky is pretty high.

You can't go in there with the expectation that they should just get over it. You decide the right behaviour is to go in with your happy face on. You bound into the restaurant with energy and enthusiasm. However, the look on your partner's face shows that they are not sharing your mood. Right away, you realise your chosen behaviour doesn't fit the context of this space. To stay true to the intent of date night, the new behaviours you exhibit must convey that you are empathetic and apologetic.

'Baby, I am so sorry I'm late. That must have been so boring to wait for me. That's not what you want to do after a long day at work. I can't apologise enough. There's no excuse. I simply just left work that little bit too late and hit peak hour. Date night is really important to me and I want us to have the best night possible. But I understand if you are angry with me and you have every right to be.'

Date night is back on track.

GRUMPY MANAGER

You are in a team meeting with your peers and the managing director, who you all report to. As he enters the room you can tell that today he has his cranky mask on. He has the last quarter figures and starts ranting and raving about the various divisions not pulling their weight. It seems that you have drawn the short straw. Your team has recently migrated to a new computer system and productivity is down because you're all still trying to get used to the new process. He starts hammering you, your results and your team. He also manages to slip in a couple of personal attacks on your leadership style.

You walk out of the room furious. You get back to your office and go over the meeting again and again. Your internal dialogue is, 'He is such an arse. He's a jerk who makes up for his shortcomings in leadership by blaming other people. He always singles me out and makes my department the scapegoat. I looked like such an idiot in front of the leadership team. Why am I such a screw-up? I hate this place.'

Suddenly you realise that you are late for a meeting with your own team.

You walk into the meeting room and just let them have it. You criticise their work ethic, intelligence and commitment. You give them a to-do list as long as your arm and tell them you want it by tomorrow. They scurry out of the room looking for a place to hide. You carry that mood home and unselfishly share it with your whole family.

Let's rewind.

Reflect

You walk out of the meeting and go to your office. 'Wow that was a complete beating. I have never seen him like that. That was out of line but I guess he has a huge amount of pressure on him to turn this company around. Actually, I have a tendency to do the same thing when I'm under pressure. He was very hard on my team, but we have been underperforming because of the system changeover. We'll get back on track once we are used to it. We are still on track if we keep delivering.'

You do your 'what went well'. 'What I was most proud of in that meeting was that I stayed calm. I didn't respond to his threats and just kept presenting him with the facts. I stood my ground and didn't let him intimidate me. I think the rest of the guys in the room will respect me for that.'

Rest

You push your meeting back ten minutes and go for a walk to shake off the adrenaline you inherited from the last meeting. You return to your office to compose yourself. You sit there for two minutes, slow your breathing rate down and focus on a sign on the building next door.

Reset

Once your mind clears you begin to focus on the next meeting. Your intention for the meeting is to establish key priorities for the next quarter. You want them walking out of the room with clarity around what are the exact steps to raise output.

You decide that the key behaviours you need to exhibit are clear communication, staying calm and being very certain of the next steps, the whole while being relaxed and confident so that your team takes on this persona. When you arrive at the meeting they inform you that it has got back to them that the managing director is furious at their department. You can tell that they are deeply concerned by this and fear for their jobs. You quickly realise that the strategic plan can wait, and what this team needs is support and reassurance. You spend the next hour actively listening to their concerns and reassuring them that they are on track to meet budget. You reschedule the meeting for tomorrow and encourage the team to switch off when they get home and not to worry about it.

AVERTING DIET DISASTER

You have been on your new lifestyle plan for the last two weeks, with great success. After an exhausting day you come home to see your roommate going out. As they leave they point out that they had a birthday at work and the rest of the cake is in the fridge. They tell you that you're welcome to finish it off. Oh no! Cake is not part of the new lifestyle plan.

As you enter the kitchen the smell reminds you of how hungry you are. You swear you can hear the cake call your name and, if you're not mistaken, it's also telling you that it is delicious and fluffy. In the blink of an eye you find yourself at the fridge with one hand on the door.

To avert a disaster, it's time to insert a Third Space.

Reflect

You focus on the fact that you have had a great day. You have been to the gym and eaten well. You quickly think of the previous times in the last two weeks that you have avoided breaking your eating plan. The story you tell yourself is that lately you have discovered that these types of food never taste as good as you think they are going to. You remind yourself that usually, after you eat them, you feel guilty for the next five hours. You remind yourself that you're no longer that person and you *always* follow through on your goals when you set them.

Rest

You pause and walk away from the fridge and sit on the lounge.

Reset

You remind yourself of the intention for your health kick. You want to get back into shape for your school reunion and get through the day with energy left to enjoy your life. You choose a new behaviour. You call your best friend to distract you from the cake. While you're talking to them you put on your runners, grab your headphones and go for a walk. Crisis averted!

I'd like to finish with one thought. Don't fall into the trap of being conditioned by the self-help world to believe that in order to have a happy and success-ful life you need to set audacious goals, turn your life upside down and change everything. You don't need to do any of that. If you want balance, better performance and happiness, pay attention to the way you move between the different roles, tasks and environments that make up your day. Forget the big stuff; pay attention to these small micro-transitions.

Now that you have all the tools you need to more smoothly and powerfully move between the many spaces that make up your life, it's over to you.

Go forth and transition.

All the best

Dr Adam Fraser

Endnotes

Preface

[1]   Lundin, S. & Hagerman, C., *Top Performer,* Hodder Mobius, 2007

[2]   Lundon, S., *FISH! A Remarkable Way to Boost Morale and Improve Results,* Hodder Paperback, 2002

Chapter 1

[1]   Gallup Consulting, 'The Gallup Q12 – Employee Engagement – Poll 2008 Results', Australian Overview, February 2009

[2]   Harter, J. & Rath, T., *Wellbeing: The Five Essential Elements,* Gallup Press, New York, 2010

[3]   Seligman, M., *Authentic Happiness,* Random House, Sydney 2002

Chapter 2

[1]   Gladwell, M., *Blink,* Penguin Books Ltd, 2006

[2]   Duxbury, L.E. & Higgins, C., 'Work-life balance in Australia in the new millennium: rhetoric versus reality', Beaton Consulting, South Yarra, 2008

[3]   Bureau of Labor Statistics, 'American time use survey 2010', Washington D.C., 2011

[4]   Bronson, P., 'How we spend our Leisure Time', *Time* magazine, October 2006

[5] Loehr, J. & Schwartz, T., *The Power of Full Engagement,* Free Press, 2005

Chapter 3

[1] Pocock, B., Skinner, N. and Ichii, R., *Work, life and workplace flexibility: the Australian work and life index 2009,* University of South Australia, 2009

[2] Hecht, T.D. & Allen, N.J., 'A longitudinal examination of the work–nonwork boundary strength construct', *Journal of Organizational Behavior,* 30 (7), 2009, pp.839–62 Kreiner, G.E., 'Consequences of work-home segmentation or integration: a person-environment fit perspective', *Journal of Organizational Behavior,* 27 (4), 2006, pp.485–507 Kossek, E.E., Lautsch, B.A. & Eaton, S.C., 'Telecommuting, control, and boundary management: Correlates of policy use and practice, job control, and work–family effectiveness', *Journal of Vocational Behavior,* 68 (2), 2006, pp.347–67

[3] Van Steenenberg, E.F. & Ellemers, N., 'Is managing the work–family interface worthwhile? Benefits for employee health and performance', *Journal of Organizational Behavior,* 30 (5), 2009, pp.617–42

[4] Hecht, T.D. & Allen, N.J., 'A longitudinal examination of the work–nonwork boundary strength construct', *Journal of Organizational Behavior,* 30 (7), 2009, pp.839–62

[5] Frone, M.R., Russell, M. & Cooper, M.L., 'Antecedents and outcomes of work family conflict: Testing a model of the work–family interface', *Journal of Applied Psychology*, 77 (1), 1992, pp.65–78

Chapter 4

[1] Molineux, J. & Fraser, A., 'The impact of positive thinking and other techniques in transition from work to home situations for reducing work–life conflict', Proceedings of the 25th Australian and New Zealand Academy of Management Conference, Wellington, NZ, 2011

Chapter 5

[1] Seligman, M. & Csikszentmihalyi, M., 'Positive psychology: An introduction', *American Psychologist*, 55, 2000, pp.5–14
[2] Gable, S.L. et al, 'What Do You Do When Things Go Right? The Intrapersonal and Interpersonal Benefits of Sharing Positive Events', *Journal of Personality and Social Psychology*, 87 (2), 2004, pp.228–45

Chapter 6

[1] Seligman, M., *Learned Optimism: How to Change Your Mind and Your Life,* Random House, Sydney, 2006

Chapter 7

[1] Clarke, A.E., Diener, E., Georgellis, Y. & Lucas, R.E., 'Lags and leads in life satisfaction: A test of the baseline hypothesis', *The Economic Journal,* 118 (529), 2008, pp.F222–F243

[2] Rosenthal, J.M. & Okie, S., 'White coat, mood indigo – depression in medical school', *New England Journal of Medicine,* 353 (11), 2005, pp.1085–88

[3] Newbury-Birch, D., White, M. & Kamali, F., 'Factors influencing alcohol and illicit drug use amongst medical students', *Drug and Alcohol Dependence,* 59 (2), 2000, pp.125–30 Webb, E., Ashton, C.H., Kelly, P. & Kamah, F., 'An update on British medical students lifestyles', *Medical Education,* 32 (3), 1998, pp.325–31

[4] Fahrenkopf, A.M., Sectish T.C., Barger L.K. et al., 'Rates of medication errors among depressed and burnt out residents: prospective cohort study', *British Medical Journal,* 336 (7642), 7 February 2008

[5] Hassed, C., *The Essence of Health: The seven pillars of wellbeing. Education, Stress Management, Spirituality, Exercise, Nutrition, Connectedness and Environment,* Ebury Press, Sydney, 2008

[6] Hassed, C., de Lisle, S., Sullivan, G. & Pier, C., 'Enhancing the health of medical students: outcomes of an integrated mindfulness and lifestyle

program', *Adv in Health Sci Edu,* 14, 2009, pp.387–98

[7]   Moses, A., '"La-la land" law: call to ban iPods and phones while crossing roads', *Sydney Morning Herald,* January 2011

[8]   Richtel, M., 'Forget Gum. Walking and Using Phone is Risky', *New York Times,* 16 January 2010

[9]   Hylton, H., 'Texting and Walking: Dangerous Mix', *Time Business,* March 2008

[10]   Beilock, S., *Choke,* Free Press, New York, 2010

[11]   Wang, J., Rao, H., Wetmore, G.S., Furlan, P.M., Korczykowski, M., Dinges, D.F. & Detre, J.A., 'Perfusion functional MRI reveals cerebral blood flow pattern under psychological stress', *Proceedings of the National Academy of Sciences of the United States of America,* 102 (49), 6 December 2005, pp.17804–9

[12]   Johnson, S., *Where Good Ideas Come From: The Natural History of Innovation,* Riverhead Hardcover, New York, 2010

[13]   Rath, T., *StrengthsFinder 2.0,* Gallup Press, New York, 2007

[14]   Killingsworth, M.A. & Gilbert, D.T., 'A wandering mind is an unhappy mind', *Science,* 330, November 2010

Chapter 8

[1]   Csikszentmihalyi, M., *Finding Flow,* Basic Books, New York, 1997

[2] Harter, J. & Rath, T., *Wellbeing: The Five Essential Elements,* Gallup Press, New York, 2010

[3] Kivimaki, M., Ferrie, J.E., Brunner, E. et al., 'Justice at work and reduced risk of coronary heart disease among employees', (AHRQ Grant HS06516), *Archives of Internal Medicine,* October 2005, pp.2245–51

[4] Harter, J.K., Schmidt, F.L., Killham E.A. & Agrawal, S., 'Q12® Meta-Analysis: The Relationship Between Engagement at Work and Organizational Outcomes', Gallup Inc., New York, August 2007

[5] Butterworth, P., Leach, L.S., Strazdins, L., Olesen, S.C., Rodgers, B. & Broom, D.H., 'The psychosocial quality of work determines whether employment has benefits for mental health: results from a longitudinal national household panel survey', *Occupational and Environmental Medicine,* 68 (11), March 2011, pp.806–12

[6] Bartel, C. & Saavedra, R., 'The Collective Construction of Work Group Moods', *Administrative Science Quarterly,* 45 (2), June 2000, pp.197–231

[7] Fowler, J.H. & Christakis, N.A., 'Dynamic spread of happiness in a large social network: Longitudinal analysis over 20 years in the Framingham heart study', *British Medical Journal,* 337, 2008, p.a2338

[8]   Christakis, N.A. & Fowler, J.H., *Connected: The surprising power of our social networks and how they shape our lives,* Little, Brown and Company, New York, 2009

Chapter 9

[1]   Wegner, D.M., 'How to Think, Say or Do Precisely the Worst Thing for Any Occasion', S *cience,* 325 (5936), 3 July 2009, pp.48–50

[2]   WorldOne, 'International Workplace Productivity Survey 2010', WorldOne [on behalf of LexisNexis], June–July 2010.

[3]   Atkinson, L., 'Pleasure and Pain', *Sydney Morning Herald,* 13 November 2008

[4]   [no author] 'First break all the rules – the charms of frugal innovation', *Economist,* 15 April 2010

[5]   Ananad, G., 'The Henry Ford of Heart Surgery – In India, a Factory Model for Hospitals Is Cutting Costs and Yielding Profits', *Wall Street Journal,* 25 November 2009

Chapter 12

[1]   Gladwell, M., *The Tipping Point,* Time Warner Books UK, 2001

[2]   Diener, E., Sandvik, E. & Pavot, W., 'Happiness is the frequency not the intensity of positive versus negative affect' with Strack, F., Argyle, M. & Schwartz, N. (eds.), *Subjective well-being:*

An interdisciplinary perspective, Pergamon Press, Oxford, England, 1991, pp.119–39

[3] Morse, G., 'The Science Behind the Smile', *Harvard Business Review,* 90 (1/2), January–February 2012

[4] Goleman, D., Boyatzis, R. & McKee, A., 'Primal Leadership – The Hidden Driver of Great Performance', *Harvard Business Review,* 79 (11), December 2001, pp.42–51

[5] Lyumbomirsky, S., King, L. & Diener, E., 'The benefits of frequent positive affect: Does happiness lead to success?', *Psychological Bulletin,* 131, 2005, pp.803–55

[6] Fredrickson, B.L., 'What good are positive emotions? Review of General Psychology', *American Psychology,* 2, 1998, pp.300–19 Fredrickson, B.L., 'The role of positive emotions in positive psychology: The broaden-and-build theory of positive emotions', *American Psychologist,* 56, 2001, pp.218–26

[7] Isen, A.M., 'Positive affect and decision making', in Lewis, M. & Haviland-Jones, J.M. (eds.), *Psychological and biological approaches to emotion,* 2000, pp.75–94

[8] Hillsdale, N.J., Erlbaum Lazarus, R.S. & Folkman, S., *Stress, Appraisal, and Coping,* Springer, New York, 1984

[9] Tomaka, J., Blascovich, J., Kelsey, R.M. & Leitten, C.L., 'Subjective, physiological, and behavioural effects of threat and challenge ap-

praisals', *Journal of Personality and Social Psychology,* 65, 1993, pp.248–60 Frederickson, B.L. & Branigan, C., 'Positive emotions broaden the scope of attention and thought action repertoires', *Cognition and Emotion,* 19, 2005, pp.803–55

[10] Waldinger, H.A. & Isaacowitz, D.M., 'Positive mood broadens visual attention to positive stimuli', *Motivation and Emotion,* 30, 2006, pp.89–101

[11] Lyubomirsky, S., King, L. & Diener, E., 'The benefits of frequent positive affect: Does happiness lead to success?', *Psychological Bulletin,* 131, 2005, 803–55

[12] Staw, B.M., Sutton, R.I. et. al., 'Employee Positive Emotion and Favorable Outcomes at the Workplace', *Organization Science,* 5 (1), February 1994, pp.51–71

[13] Staw, B.M. & Barsade, S.G., 'Affect and managerial performance: A test of the sadder-but-wiser vs. happier-and-smarter hypothesis', *Administrative Science Quarterly,* 38, 1993, pp.304–31

[14] Kopelman, S., Rosette, A.S. & Thompson, L., 'The three faces of Eve: Strategic displays of positive, negative and neutral emotions in negotiations', *Organizational Behavior and Human Decision Processes,* 99 (1), January 2006, pp.81–101

[15]   Frederickson, B.L. & Braingan, C., 'Positive emotions broaden the scope of attention and thought action repertoires', *Cognition and Emotion,* 19, 2005, pp.313–32

Acknowledgements

This section is the most fun part to write of any book. It's my chance to get mushy and tell those in my life how much they mean to me.

First, to my speaking mentor Doug Malouf, you're an extraordinary man who saved me from a life of being stuck in a lab. Thanks for starting me on this crazy safari. I have had a ball.

John Tilden, without your support, guidance and wisdom my career could not be where it is today. You're a good man.

To Matt Church, your Thought Leaders program was a launch pad that gave me the skills to create this book. You have done more to drive Thought Leadership than the rest of us could ever hope for. To Peter Sheahan, thanks for forcing me to be better and dragging me forward with your tsunami of certainty. Will you ever forgive me for *that* speech I made at your wedding?

To my business manager, Julie 'Step Back' Winterbottom. You are my hero and I aspire each day to be more and more like you. Thanks for putting up with my neuroticism. You are a class act on all levels. Don't worry, one day you will get that pony and until then, ninja school will have to do.

To all the O2 team – Rach, Becs, Heidi and Leanne you are always there when I need you. Thank you for believing in what we do wholeheartedly.

Chris Helder, thanks for getting my edits back in record time and showing me what amazing complexity lies in simplicity. You have an immeasurable gift. It's a pleasure to watch you in action. Heyyyyyy Barcelona!!!

To Dan Gregory, you made me look at this concept through a different lens. I can't thank you enough. Still jealous of your brain! Marty Wilson, you are a genius. You added flair and humour to help the book come alive. I owe you big time. Sue Lindsay, you have been an amazing friend and a constant source of support and inspiration. You are the most talented consultant I have ever met. To Muz, thanks for being the best friend anyone could wish for. We grew up together and I would not be the person I am today if you hadn't come along. Look forward to growing old and watching our girls play in the front yard. To my office manager Kristina Still, thanks for doing all the edits and being a willing soundboard every time I had a new idea or lacked confidence. You are easily the hardest working and most competent person I have ever had the pleasure to work with. But would you please stop bringing lamingtons to work?

To my literary agent Mary Cunnane, thanks for believing in this project and fighting so hard for it to find the right home. Thanks to all the team at Random House Australia for giving *The Third Space* its physical form.

To the irrepressible Jennifer Sheahan. As usual, you did a great job of the design. Sorry for all the late night Skype calls and tight deadlines. Thank you most of all for bringing great wine every time you come over for dinner.

When you start out in a new career, it is important to have people who believe in you more than you do yourself. Thanks to Winsome Bernard, Emma Isaacs, Amber Fullerton, Olivia Ruello and Avril Henry. It's a true sign of friendship when people do things for you despite there being nothing in it for them. A special mention must go to Deborah Claxton and Sharmila Nanha. Not only do you drive my business and champion me to the world, your charm and profession-alism make doing work with you both an absolute pleasure.

To all my clients, to the tens of thousands of people who I have presented to, and to the hundreds who have sent me emails to keep me updated on their progress: you gave me the material to write this book. I learn more and more from you all every day.

To my family – Dougie, Di, Sammy and Doris. You have always been there and you remain an incredible source of support and love. I hope this makes you proud. To my dog Tilly, thanks for snoring at my feet while I wrote the book. One should never write alone. I also appreciated the lack of judgement when I read it out aloud to you.

To my wife Chris, you are my 'super girl'. You picked up the slack at home while I was writing this book without a single complaint. You are the most amazing wife and mother, and Isabella and I are lucky to have you and the joy you bring to our lives. It is a privilege to wake up next to you each day.

Finally, to Isabella, my little 'pumpkin'. You taught me the reason that we should want to be deeply present in each moment.

FURTHER INFORMATION ON THIRD SPACE RESEARCH

My research into the impact of the Third Space on a company's profit, culture and productivity is still underway. Any companies interested in being involved in this research can email me at business@dradamfr aser.com.

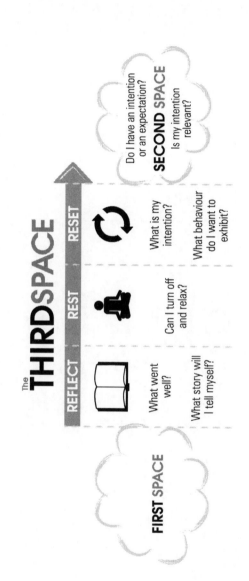

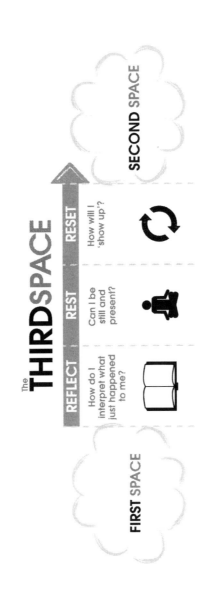

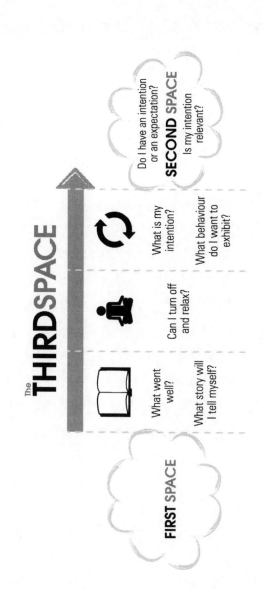

Back Cover Material

Do you ever wish you could

- get over a bad day at work and not take it out on your partner or children?
- put a personal disagreement behind you and show up for work ready to engage your team?
- endure a demotivating meeting or experience, but still approach your next task positively and enthusiastically?

Every day we undertake dozens of different roles, tasks and experiences. Most of us habitually carry our mindset and emotional state from one of these activities to the next – and all too often this has negative, occasionally disastrous consequences.

For years we've been told it's getting the 'big' stuff right that gives us balance and makes us happy: the holidays, the audacious goals, the pay rises. But in our hearts we know it's really the small stuff: a great result at work, our welcome home, an absorbing conversation, a game with the kids.

This book is all about getting the small stuff **right** – not 'sweating' it, but making it much more rewarding, much more often. It's about using the 'Third Space' (that moment of transition between a first activity and the second that follows it), to mentally 'show up' right for whatever comes next. Gaining control of the Third Space will **empower** you to do this any time and every time. You will consistently be your best for your work, your family, your friends and yourself – and you will find that the key to **balance** and **happiness** was always there waiting for you in the **Third Space.**

Books For ALL Kinds of Readers

At ReadHowYouWant we understand that one size does not fit all types of readers. Our innovative, patent pending technology allows us to design new formats to make reading easier and more enjoyable for you. This helps improve your speed of reading and your comprehension. Our EasyRead printed books have been optimized to improve word recognition, ease eye tracking by adjusting word and line spacing as well as minimizing hyphenation. Our EasyRead SuperLarge editions have been developed to make reading easier and more accessible for vision-impaired readers. We offer Braille and DAISY formats of our books and all popular E-Book formats.

We are continually introducing new formats based upon research and reader preferences. Visit our web-site to see all of our formats and learn how you can Personalize our books for yourself or as gifts. Sign up to Become A (RHYW) Registered Reader.

www.readhowyouwant.com

13922007R00201

Printed in Great Britain
by Amazon.co.uk, Ltd.,
Marston Gate.